*This book is dedicated to Corey Anton, love of my life.*

# SEX, ETHICS, AND COMMUNICATION

**Valerie V. Peterson**

*Grand Valley State University*

San Diego, CA

First published in the United States of America in 2011 by Cognella, a division of University Readers, Inc.

Trademark Notice: Product or corporate names may be trademarks or registered trademarks, and are used only for identification and explanation without intent to infringe.


15 14 13 12 11          1 2 3 4 5

Printed in the United States of America


ISBN: 978-1-60927-025-4

www.cognella.com  800.200.3908

# Contents

Acknowledgments                                          1

Introduction                                             3

## Part I: Ethics

Sexual Failure and Sexual Responsibility                13

The Sex Ethics                                          21

The Sex Ethics Diagram                                 35

Vulnerability                                           39

Comments About Categories                              47

Why Statistics Are Useless for Ethics                  51

## Part II: Communication

Sex As Communication                                   59

Communicating Interpersonally About Sex                63

Communicating Publicly about Sex:                      71
Metaphors and Narratives
  The Gatekeeper                                        75
  The Duck Pond Game                                    79

Editing Sexual Practice     82
Get a Grip     84
For Singles: I Don't Date     87

Making Good Sex More Likely     91

# Part III: Society

Children     99

Innocence vs. Experience     103

Family     107

Two Out of Three     111

Eighty Cents' Worth     115

Sex and Politics     119

Marriage     125

On Same-Sex Marriage     129

*Appendix A: Euphemisms and Alternative Wording Suggestions*     *135*

*Appendix B: Sex Inventory*     *139*

*Works Cited*     *143*

# Acknowledgments

I would like to thank Grand Valley State University for the generous post-tenure sabbatical, during which the majority of this book was written. I also wish to thank faculty at the University of Iowa who supported my study of sex and sexuality while I was a doctoral student there. Bruce E. Gronbeck gave me helpful feedback on my dissertation—a rhetorical and cultural analysis of popular sex manuals, and he made sure I kept my focus on the discursive elements of sexuality. Some ideas in this book are those he told me I could not include in that earlier project. Leslie Margolin helped teach me how to write about sexuality by generously sharing his own work in progress and letting a classmate and me participate in the editing process. Leslie Baxter offered useful insights into scholarly writing and professionalism. Barbara Welch-Breder encouraged me to study the relationship between communication, sex, and sexuality at the outset of my studies, and helped me feel less awkward about taking on these very challenging territories of concern. Over the years and at a number of different institutions, Fred Antczak has provided moral support, encouraged and supported my research, and helped me grow as a teacher and thinker. Other scholars who played a role in my early studies of sexuality, and who have supported my research efforts, include Helen Sterk, John Waite Bowers, Donovan Ochs, John Lyne, Randy Hirokawa, John Durham Peters, Bernard and Sue Duffy, Michael Calvin McGee, Mary Trachsel, David Depew, Sharon Crowley, and Takis Poulakos.

Then there are all the colleagues, friends, relatives, students, and acquaintances with whom I've conversed on the topics of sex and sexuality.

Their thoughts, article and book suggestions, and constructive criticisms have made an undertaking such as this much more possible. In so many instances, I have been informed, surprised, enlightened, and impressed by what people say; what they're willing to say; and how much there is to know. Students in my fall 2009 special topics course (Rhetorics of Sex and Sexuality) gave me hope that there might be interest in a book such as this, and helped me update and expand upon some of my insights. Allison Forrest, a student in my Vision and Culture class, turned my sex ethics diagram into an attractive poster suitable for public presentations. Colleagues who study sexuality, masculinity, communication, and/or related topics also have been profoundly helpful to my thinking, especially Teresita Garza, Brent Malin, Natalie Sydorenko, and Robert MacDougall. Two colleagues in particular, Joey Pogue and Ann Byars, were instrumental in the later stages of this project. Their enthusiasm for my ideas literally kept me going when the going was tough. I would also like to thank my colleagues in the GVSU School of Communications; my "Old Mission" neighbors; my wonderful friends; my sister; my extended family; my inspirational grandmother, Artemis; my life partner, colleague, intellectual sounding board, and husband, Corey Anton; and my awesome and incredible parents Aris and Grace Peterson, for their kindness, moral support, helpful ideas, constructive criticism, good humor, and love.

# Introduction

With mantras like "just do it," "just say no," and "show me the money," the 1990s did little to prepare people in the United States to be thoughtful about sexual relations. The first decade of the 2000s has been no more helpful. Abstinence-only sex education offered by public schools has affected behavior somewhat, but STDs continue to proliferate, and unintended teen pregnancy rates are on the rise in many populations. Divorce is still pervasive, and the "dating scene" is increasingly confounding and complex. Electronic information exchange and virtual reality portend a new world of matchmaking possibilities and alternative entertainments, but often promise more than they can deliver. At the same time, wholesome, non-commercialized spaces—or even just safe spaces—where people can spend time together and get to know each other seem to be dwindling.

Drugs and the hyper-sexualized mass media do not help matters. Drug abuse, particularly the abuse of alcohol, ecstasy, date-rape drugs, and various street drugs and pharmaceuticals, numbs people to the ethics of sexual matters by allowing the excuse of intoxication or chemical alteration for either irresponsible actions, or mindless passivity. Print, visual, and electricity-powered mass media (including popular health and beauty magazines, TV shows, feature films, cartoons, comic books, advertisements, pornography, and numerous Internet outlets) offer images, easy formulas and sex roles, a power- and envy-driven star culture, questionable norms of behavior, and often warped values that undermine human decency by reducing people, bodies, and sex to commodities.

Religions—including Catholicism, with its strict rules about masturbation, contraception, and abortion—find themselves facing a whole new collection of sexual ethical dilemmas made possible by fertility drugs, new and improved reproductive technologies, and the electronic age. The fundamentalist notion of being "born again" so as to wipe clean the slate of past activities, including sexual activities, may seem an attractive idea for those who did not wait until marriage to have sex (but wish they had), or for a variety of other real or imagined sexual transgressions. But asking God for forgiveness does little to right any wrongs done to past partners and other affected parties, nor does it necessarily or easily solve future sexual, ethical, and communicative quandaries. As always, religious doctrines, laws policing sex and sexuality, reproductive technology, reproductive rights, marriage laws, family laws, and economic policies exist as battlegrounds of sexual/political power, with profound personal implications. In the face of all this, and as long as human-embodied sexuality is still a desirable practice, people of this generation and the next will need to make sense of the complicated ethical terrain of sex and sex relations with nuance and honesty—not slogans and excuses.

Times like these call for an ethic of sex that can be applied regardless of procreative intentions. This book is a response to this call. It is written for people concerned about the ethics of interpersonal (two-person) sexual relations. It is also written for those concerned with the ways people make sense of sexual relations and the ways people communicate about these relations in their everyday conversations, and in the broader culture.

This book does not address virtual sex, distance sex, cyborg/cyber sex, or post-humanism. On the contrary, the concern is same-space/time interactions that are primarily "of the flesh." The book is somewhat more directed toward heterosexual readers (e.g., it discusses contraception and unintended pregnancy as consequences of sexual activity), but it is not limited to these readers. Intentional use of gender-neutral wording throughout the text allows many observations and examples to apply equally well to lesbian, gay, and/or other sexual relations or relationships.

This book also owes something to my academic career, in which I have, among other things, studied sex and sexuality, and the ways sex and sexuality are discussed in a number of popular contexts.[1] Some of my scholarly writings critique the metaphors, mythologies, narratives, and other rhetorical elements of popular sex manuals, TV shows, and theatrical performances.[2] While artifacts of popular culture like these tell us little about what people actually *do* sexually, they offer a window into assumptions, expectations, and ideals of sex and sexual practice. In studying these texts, I have become familiar with theories of sex and sexuality spanning intellectual territories such as anthropology, philosophy, sociology, psychology, political science, cultural studies, communication studies, feminism and women's studies, gender studies, masculinity studies, queer theory, biology, and behavioral science.

As a college professor, I have learned about sex and sexuality as it relates to the lives of my students. Across almost 20 years of teaching practical and theoretical communication studies courses, I have helped students of all ages and from a wide variety of backgrounds craft speeches and papers on topics such as sexually transmitted diseases; love, adoption and abortion; marriage; sexual orientation and discrimination; Internet infidelity; and other sex- and sexuality-related topics. Sometimes these speeches and papers get personal. In one case, a male student gave a speech about masculinity, his mother's experience of rape, and its effect on their lives. A female student (and mother of two) gave a speech about her choice to abort an unintended pregnancy that jeopardized her life. Another female student spoke in praise of her son, a product of date rape. Another student wrote a paper about the metaphor "marriage is work" and its implications. In one instance, I encouraged a student who wanted to persuade his audience that "a fetus is a person" to give a "why people should wait until marriage to have sex" speech instead, as a more potentially effective "pro-life" argument (and it went over quite well, despite—or perhaps partly because—he was willing to "out" himself as a virgin). While not directly related to sex, media images of women, poor body image, and troubles with eating disorders are related to bodies and matters of power, relationship, and control. Speeches and papers about these are also common. Every year, I learn something new.

Students have also shared their experiences in other ways. In class-room discussions, and as their lives unfold over the course of the semester, students often share insights into sex and sexuality, and grapple with sex- and sexuality-related issues. In doing so, they share information, both good and bad, that they might not share with even close friends or family members. One year, a student came to my office to tell me of her just-discovered unintended pregnancy (the result of a broken condom and her first try at sex with her boyfriend). Another student wrote me a note saying she decided to acknowledge her own date-rape experience after an in-class discussion that included the topic. I even had a student tell his classmates of a party he threw, where he took a drunk and passed-out freshman girl into a back room, keeping her there under watch so she could be safe until she woke up (a safeguarding effort I publicly sup-ported). In these instances, I did not advertise myself as a counselor (nor was I asked to be one). I was, however, exposed to ethical dilemmas that deserve real attention.

Much of what I have seen and heard from students, from friends and family, and in the larger culture worries me. With all the sex and sexuality in the media, and with all the talk about it, I see little concern for other people, little concern about right and wrong, and hardly any discussion of self-discipline and ethical judgment as virtues. When "good sex" is mentioned, it usually means simply "pleasurable sex," and is often either reminisced about as a vague memory, or as a taboo or unreachable fantasy ideal. On the other hand, ethical sex (that is, sex that is good from an ethical perspective), is largely equated with marital and intentionally pro-creative sex. But this latter type of sex is not particularly common, even in most marriages. What I am interested in are ways people might be "good" about sex—ways they might have "better," rather than "worse," sex. By this I mean sex that is ethically informed, and is, at the same time, part of the wider range of sexuality and sexual practices common to everyday life.

In this book, I bring the concern about good sex center stage, ap-proaching the subjects of sex, ethics, and communication as a liberal humanist. Among other things, taking a liberal humanist approach means that no particular religious doctrine or dogma determines my approach, although there is no doubt my upbringing, my experiences with religion, my education, and my teaching have all informed my perspective and helped deepen my sense of the richness and value of humanity. As a liberal of the classical sort, I believe free will and self-discipline are preferable to blindly following doctrine, even if the outcome of the latter seems simpler and safer. But I in no way equate liberality with license. I believe we humans are a special kind of being, ones capable of cultivating concern for others and making good choices for ourselves. With free will comes the need to develop healthy self-discipline, and from this grows maturity and the capacity to make good choices in the future. While many and varied subjects are relevant to the study of sex and sexuality (including economic forces such as poverty and excessive wealth, and social forces such as media images, religious doctrines, advice manuals, etc.), this book focuses mainly on individuals, their freedom and responsibility to others, and to themselves. Such a focus highlights cases where people have some choices and some control in their lives—instances where ethical decision making can occur.

Some people fear that paying attention to sex and sexuality might "ruin" it, and they would rather not discuss it or think about it. This book is not for these people. Sexual activities of the sort discussed in the following pages involve at least two people, and other people are at least peripherally involved in the matter (e.g., children, potential children, family members, friends, etc.). This makes sex a social act—albeit a unique kind of social act—and the social world is an ethical world. There are important human consequences to social actions, and there are better ways and worse ways to handle situations. Sometimes it is unclear what is the better thing to do and what is the worse thing to do in a situation, especially when there are competing values, but we as humans are capable of moral reasoning. *It is our responsibility, in social situations, to try to do less, rather than greater, amounts of harm to others. It is also worthwhile to try to do less, rather than greater, amounts of harm to ourselves.* Writing this statement and putting it in italics doesn't make ethical dilemmas any easier to solve, but it does at least articulate the politics behind this book.

There are times when it is more and less appropriate to talk about sex. There are ways to talk about sex that are better, rather than worse. It is wise to address issues and concerns about sex and sexuality before sexual activity occurs, and also during and after sexual activity. Anyone not willing to address important matters before sex, during sex, or after sex is a risk—and at risk. Anyone willing to address important matters before sex, during sex, or after sex takes a step toward being responsible (and perhaps also toward better sexual relations). It is also important to consider how sex is depicted in popular metaphors, myths, and narratives, because the ways people think and talk about sex can (re)shape existing understandings. And finally, it is important to consider how sex plays a part in various contexts in society (e.g., reproductive rights, marriage, family, the economy, politics), so that we can better understand the world in which we find ourselves. In all these instances, willingness to address sexual matters makes a person more of a lover: that is, more of a loving person, rather than less of one.

Accordingly, this book is divided into three parts. *Part I: Ethics* includes chapters addressing sexuality as an ethical practice—a practice that is related to, but not reducible to, communication. These chapters discuss sexual responsibility, sex ethics (rationales/justifications for having sex), and vulnerability. They offer cautionary comments about easy categories and amoral statistics.

*Part II: Communication* then considers the many ways that sex and communication are related. The first chapter explains how sex itself can serve *as a form of* communication. The next chapter addresses ways to communicate interpersonally *about* sex, and refers readers to "Appendix A: Euphemisms and Alternative Wording Suggestions." The following chapters explore metaphors and narratives of sex that might make useful alternatives to the ways sex and sexuality are often depicted in public discourse. Part II closes with a chapter, "Making Good Sex More Likely," and refers the reader to "Appendix B: Sex Inventory"—a list of sex-, ethics-, and communication-related questions readers may want to periodically ask themselves—drawn from Parts I and II.

In *Part III: Society*, contexts where sex and sexuality loom large are discussed. Family, abortion, children, marriage, economics, and politics are just a few of the topics addressed in chapters designed to show how sex is part of the larger institutions and situations in which we find ourselves, and thus part of any changes we would want to make to those institutions or those situations.

I take sole responsibility for the content of this book. I think readers should bring a healthy skepticism to all writings on sex/sexuality, and for that matter, all writings on any important subject. I do ask readers to treat this book as a whole, even if they read only one or a few chapters at a time, or find only one or a few chapters of interest. Statements on sensitive topics can be easily misconstrued when taken out of context, and there are instances in this book when arguments in later chapters rely upon groundwork laid in preceding chapters (i.e., discussions of sexual practice rely on previous discussions of the ethical necessity of birth control). This is why I begin the book with ethics, and then move on to other subjects. Hopefully, readers will carry ideas forward as they go.

I have tried to qualify my statements enough so that I don't appear to pretend to know everything about sex and intimacy. Where I fail, I ask for the reader's forgiveness and sympathy.

## Endnotes

1. Valerie V. Peterson, on press, 2010, 2001, 1998.
2. Valerie V. Peterson, 2008, 2005, 2002, 2000, 1999.

# Part I
## Ethics

# Sexual Failure and
# Sexual Responsibility

Historically, cultures, religions, tribes, and families have tried to make sexual failure, or "sin," simple. They have tried to make it easy for people to know what the "wrong" kinds of sexual practice are, so that these practices can be easily avoided. These practices have included (but are not limited to) the following:

- sex before a certain age
- sex before marriage
- sex with a child or sibling
- sex with a stranger/strangers
- sex with animals (bestiality)
- sex that is forced
- sex for (or by means of) money
- too much sex or not enough sex
- adultery
- polygamy
- sex with someone of the same sex
- this or that particular arrangement or use of bodies and/or body parts, etc

Because sexual intimacy involves touch and other intimate forms of sensory perception, and because there is much at stake (possible pregnancy, possible transmission of disease, feelings and emotions) it is a particularly "real" and intense experience. While seeing and hearing are both experienced "as" and "at" a distance, touch (being touched) and active touching (feeling someone or something) involve direct contact and the added pleasures and dangers that come with human contact. Unlike vision, where humans can close their eyes or selectively attend to only portions of the visual field, touch has no distance. Unlike hearing, which can't be avoided, touching requires active engagement. Touch—and taste and smell, for that matter—are senses that require both shared space and shared time. This means that, unlike activities involving mainly hearing and seeing, sexual intimacy, which involves touch, is much more immediate. In addition, touch confirms the reality of what is seen, offers its own "vision" through the combination of feeling and movement, and can result in significant physical consequences for those who venture into its intimate practice.[1] For these and other reasons, it makes sense for cultures to have rules and laws about sex and sex-related practices, especially those practices that are violent or exploitative. It is also clear that some rules are often unevenly applied across populations, serve contestable ideological goals, and vary from time to time and culture to culture.

To be ethical about sex, people need to do more than simply obey rules. Sometimes, to be ethical, people may even need to question the sexual rules of their culture. This is because sexual norms vary across time and place, and because sexual activity presents more situations where judgment is needed than simple maxims of conduct can address. The larger context of sexual activity also often brings conflicting values into play, and weighing these values requires thoughtfulness and judgment. Completely rule-abiding people, trained to have sex only in certain specified ways and under certain conditions, might seem ethical, especially if their behavior is the same as those who carefully think about and decide upon their actions. But simple rule-followers are more likely to be at a loss when sexual intimacy presents dilemmas where many and competing values come into conflict. Without denying other meanings of sexual activity (e.g., species survival), and granting exceptions of number beyond the scope of this discussion (e.g., orgies), sexual activity is an interpersonal encounter with ethical implications. This means, to the degree culture allows, sexual activity can be as rich or as impoverished, as deep or as shallow, as the people involved make it.

In interpersonal interaction, one failure in particular stands out as the most serious failure of all: the failure to care. The failure to care is the failure to "love your neighbor as yourself." Loving your neighbor as yourself is not the same thing as "doing unto others as you would have them do unto you" (which is actually a commerce-based "doing an equivalent thing back" sort of response). Loving your neighbor is not about fair-trade value, it's about *doing what is right by and for the other person.*[2] The failure to care is the basis of some of the sexual "failures/sins" listed above (for instance, if you promise to be monogamous in marriage, then it would be wrong to be sexually intimate with someone who is not your spouse). But failure to care is not as simplistic as maxims about the behaviors listed above. Failure to care governs a much wider range of action.

The extremes of failure to care are more easily identified and more clearly unethical. Violent, forced, and coerced sex acts are the most egregious instances of failure to care (or desire to harm), especially when there are negative cultural consequences for the victimized person, in addition to the initial abuse. Imposed upon both males and females, often practiced in war, and related to anger and hatred, the desire for or lack of power, ethical disability (psychopathology, sociopathology), hostility toward a particular class of persons, and other factors, forced sex and forced sex-related acts are some of the clearest instances of failure to care. Despite the extreme nature of these failures, variations of response exist among cultures and subcultures. Some cultures, for example, are more offended and concerned by (or willing to recognize) the sexual abuse of women than they are the sexual abuse of men, the poor, slaves, the mentally ill, etc.

Coercive sex with physically and emotionally vulnerable persons is related to the failures to care just mentioned, and is a more difficult territory of meaning to navigate, especially after the fact. Date rape, incest, nursing care facility abuses, sex with a minor, medical abuses, and other instances of failure to care for vulnerable others are included in this category. Because the degree to which actions are unwelcome and persons are (considered) vulnerable varies (for instance, the cut-off age between childhood and adulthood varies by state in the United States, as well as across cultures), and because some people and cultures look more to the past while others look more to the future, responses to these kinds of sexual encounters can exist for participants/victims/survivors along a continuum ranging from mild to traumatic.

Another extreme failure to care is the failure to use contraceptives when pregnancy is unwelcome. Sex has been increasingly distanced from marriage and procreation by effective and available contraception, by the women's and gay liberation movements, and by the legal recognition of women's reproductive rights. While efforts to roll back these and other technological and social developments continue, their effects are already woven into the economic fabric of this country and in the way men and women live their lives, including the sexual intimacies in which many people engage. To some extent, contraception and reproductive rights have made it easier for men and women to have sex both before marriage and outside of marriage. This is part of the reason for the decline in prostitution over the past century.[3] But simply trading the problem of prostitution for another set of sexual practices and problems does not in any way address the ethical quandaries that people face when recreational sex is regularly practiced without protection from pregnancy and disease. On the other hand, conservative political efforts do little to take us back to earlier times or erase the effects of reproductive technologies and social change.

Where contraceptives are readily available, ethical sex demands their use in any sexual encounter that might result in pregnancy, unless pregnancy is desired and perhaps also adequately anticipated (e.g., emotionally, socially, and/or financially). If having a child is not desired, every effort should be taken to prevent pregnancy. If contraception is unavailable, sex should be put off or avoided. If it is unclear whether or not contraceptive methods will be effective, backup methods should be used. Still, contraceptives sometimes fail. If two people differ in their beliefs about what to do in the face of an unwanted pregnancy, they should reconsider engaging in any sexual activity that might result in pregnancy.

Another extreme failure to care is the failure to protect a partner (and oneself) against sexually transmitted diseases. Every era has had its sex-related and sexually transmitted diseases (STDs), and many of these diseases have been incurable and deadly. A hundred years ago, the well-known and incurable STD was syphilis. One of the biggest sex-related problems today worldwide is HIV/AIDS. The United States also has a problem with HIV/AIDS. Despite recent advances in medical science, people in this country still die from AIDS, and treatments to slow the progress of the disease are costly and complicated. Genital warts (HPV) have been around for thousands of years. In some cases, HPV can lead to cervical cancer, and if left untreated can cause death. Other diseases, such as hepatitis, herpes, and chlamydia are also dangerous, and bring their own share of physical and emotional miseries. Some STDs are hardly detectable in men, but take a significant toll on women's bodies. Many STDs cause those who have them pain, shame, expense, and/or personal loss. Governmental attention to disease comes and goes, prices of drugs fall and rise, public health services appear and disappear, and with them infection rates decrease and increase. Chances of exposure and infection vary by region, class, or other demographics, but it may take only one encounter with an afflicted person to join their ranks.

Maintaining vigilance over time against the transmission of sex-related disease is difficult, because people are embarrassed by disease, can get lazy, and do not want to live with fear. The use of condoms and other barrier methods of contraception, while sometimes essential to an ethical sexual encounter, can be aesthetically unappealing. This is not simply because of the awkwardness and qualities of latex, but also because the use of a condom results in distance, and also a sense of distance, between people. Sex is often more than a simple act to release tension or populate the earth; it can be an intimate act, an act of contact, and an expression of affection or love. Because barrier methods of contraception can interfere with that contact and that intimacy, or remind some people that they are not engaged in a particularly caring kind of intimacy, or because barrier methods require care or concern for a partner (a care or concern which may be absent in more casual contexts), people may avoid using them, and then later regret it.

The spread of STDs may never be adequately curtailed, but being honest about them, and also being honest about having them, ultimately helps rather than hurts matters. So does using appropriate protection. So does reducing one's own sexual mixing and mingling. Moving quickly from one sex partner to the next, and then the next, suggests a lack of care for the self and others. If there is any reason to do so (for example, if there are any symptoms, or if there is any reason to suspect a partner of cheating), people should have themselves checked for STDs. People should also be checked for STDs before becoming sexually active with any new partner (or having a baby—especially if passing the STD on to the baby or other injury could be avoided by treating the STD). If a new partner is unwilling to be checked for STDs, especially if this person has or seems to have a longer rather than shorter sexual history, intimate sex relations with that person (those involving the transmission of bodily fluids) should be carefully considered. Having an STD should not necessarily disqualify a person from future sexual intimacy, and no person should be blamed or punished for having or getting an STD (though they could be accused of ethical failure if getting an STD was the consequence of breaking a promise of fidelity). Love is bigger and more powerful than any disease, and people, couples, families, and friends can deal with an STD if they are willing. The more honesty there is about STDs, the better off we all are.

Another extreme of failure to care, and one related to the failures mentioned above, is lying. A person may lie by saying birth control is being (properly) used (or sterility is a fact) when it is not. Or, people may lie about (or not own up to) their marital status, or their potential or known STD(s), or their age (particularly if under the age of legal consent). Being dishonest about feelings, intentions, or the significance or status of a relationship are other examples of lying. In all of these cases, lying can lead to anger, suffering, and regret.

Hypocrisy is a special form of failure to care—a kind of lying to one's self. Hypocrites are people who say one thing but mean or do another, or who say they support or denounce one thing, but then act in ways that indicate otherwise. For example, a man who lives in the United States and says he is pro-life would need to follow certain customs in order to avoid being called a hypocrite. If this man never had sex outside of marriage and supported bringing every child he helped conceive into the world, then he should not be called a hypocrite (except perhaps by those who deny husbands all rights in decisions regarding progeny). The man's actions are sensitive to the culture in which he finds himself (one where marriage grants certain rights to husbands along with certain responsibilities) and are less likely to lead to abortion (consistent with his stated beliefs). If, in some circumstance, his wife were to choose to have an abortion, we would not call the man a hypocrite. We might even call him a victim.

On the other hand, if a man lives in the United States and says he is pro-life, but has (or has had) unprotected sex with women before or outside of marriage, he could be called a hypocrite. This is because the burden of care for children in our country is currently placed on mothers, and fathers who are not husbands have fewer rights and less say regarding their progeny. The second man's actions are more likely to lead (or have led) to abortion(s), especially if his politics differed from those of his non-marital sexual partners. In this case, it would be hypocritical for the man to call himself pro-life.

Hypocrisy is related to inauthenticity and delusion, and is so typical as to be largely ignored. And yet, despite how common it is, hypocrisy is the one contradiction of life that we have the most ability to avoid, because it is the one contradiction that begins and ends in the individual. Acting according to our stated beliefs and values is one important way to be responsible to the other people in our lives, especially those with whom we are sexually intimate.

Other instances of failure to care are also potentially damaging, and have to do with "gray areas" of intimacy. Using drugs or alcohol to the point where volition is questionable and regret likely increases misunderstand-ing and confusion both during and after sex. Neglecting or intentionally remaining confused about (or ignorant of) the sexual needs and desires of a partner (or even of one's self) is another failure to care. Over time, this can leave people feeling frustrated, slighted, and ignored.

Failing to care, lying, being a hypocrite, gray areas—these are the fail-ures that underlie most interpersonal failures, including sexual failures. Unlike a simple list of rules or maxims, the ethic of caring for others requires cultural and interpersonal sensitivity and judgment, and large amounts of attention, often more than people have or think they could have. It is a challenge to care, just as it is a challenge to see ourselves and the world around us as they are, instead of as we wish them to be. And yet this sobering project is the means by which people grow in their humanity and their understanding. To do otherwise is to do an injustice to the people around us and the people with whom we are intimate.

# The Sex Ethics

S exual intimacies are usually justified in one or more of the following ways: it feels good physically, it is consensual, I like the person I'm having sex with, I love the person I'm having sex with, I'm married to the person I'm having sex with, and I'm/we're trying to have a baby.[4] This discussion of sex rationales, or "ethics," considers the current climate of sex relations, and the contexts in which they may occur. It is based on the assumption that it is important to do right by a sexual partner and to do right by oneself, regardless of which ethic or ethics are the context of sexual relations. For people who don't wait until marriage or for those who do, for people who marry or who explicitly commit themselves to each other and want to stay monogamous, for people who were married and are now divorced and single again, for people who never marry but want a sex life, and for all those people who want to do right by others in a variety of sexually intimate relations and relationships, these rationales or ethics of sex offer ways to think about what would be the better, rather than the worse, sexual thing to do considering the situation.

## Feels Good

A healthy orgasm and the physical pleasures that come from sex are some of the things that make sexual intimacy worth having. In this ethic, the senses and pleasures derived through the senses are the focus. While sensory pleasures can't be removed from their social context in any real sense, we can make an analytical (mental) category out of them, for the purpose of thinking more pointedly about pleasure. This means the issue here is not those pleasures that come from the interpersonal or psychological or social significance of an act (e.g., "she kissed me—I feel so good because she must love me!" or "she kissed me—I feel so good because she's probably going to have sex with me soon!"). Instead, the issue is those feelings and sensations that may or may not be heightened by mental state or context, but that can be described as feeling good in a purely physical way (that is, "she kissed me—and my body/lips/skin felt good.") Other examples of "feels good" might include a warm hand on cool flesh, the tingle of a touch, the sensations of an orgasm, etc.

Sometimes, sex and sexual acts are desired solely or primarily for sensual reasons (and this can be for good or ill, depending on the context). Sex can result in a release of physical tension and a focus on the body. Sometimes, there may be a temporary and welcome loss of self (a pleasure that dissolves typical boundaries between self/other/world). In a world where gratification of the body is often denied, deferred, or channeled into unhealthy eating habits, compulsive exercise, video games, virtual relationships, or other compensatory behaviors, sexual activity of various kinds offers alternative physical outlets with potentially positive implications. Among other things, sexual activity can raise heart rate, increase blood flow, release endorphins, exercise muscles, reduce stress, and stimulate mental activity.

While sex that brings pleasure can be desirable, sex that causes pain usually is not. Rape is the clearest example of this, and it is unacceptable even if one person enjoys how it feels. Sex acts may also cause pain because of disease, virginity, injury, the effects of medications, lack of preparatory activity, or a mismatch in fit. In these cases, people may need to slow down, pursue less uncomfortable alternatives, engage in more extensive sexual play, use a lubricant, seek out medical attention, or put off/avoid sex altogther. Sometimes sex acts are painful due to undiagnosed medical conditions, the effects of medications, lack of preparatory activity, and/or other factors. Pain can be addressed by seeking medical attention, engaging in more extensive sexual play, or by using a lubricant.

While physical pleasure is desirable, much of how we experience and interpret physical interaction is colored by other factors—factors that go beyond the "feels good" rationale. As soon as we become part of the social world, we learn to respond not only to sensations, but to the contexts, roles, and norms related to these sensations. This is why children are taught early on about where on their bodies they are and are not supposed to be touched, and why men who have been conditioned against same-sex sexual relations may respond well to sexual intimacies shared with a transvestite or transsexual, until they realize their partner is not a female (or was not originally physically "designed" female). While physical pleasure is not some simple, basic, or "natural" element of sexuality that can be relied upon to guide behavior, pain is often a good indicator of what not to do.

## Consent

For many people and cultures, only consenting sexual relations are ethically acceptable. This is not simply a matter of physical pleasure and pain. It is also a psychological and emotional matter. Consent is an issue of free will, a liberty many people believe in quite dearly and expect to exercise.

Consent is not itself a simple matter, since there is somewhat of a continuum of willingness to engage in sexual relations, and some practical factors to consider as well. If one person in a sexual encounter is not awake or conscious, if their judgments about sex are compromised by alcohol or drugs or both, or if they implicitly or explicitly express that they do not want to participate in a sex act, then sexual activity with that person should not occur. If a person's consent is unclear or unstable, or if the reasons for the consent are wrongheaded, then sexual activities are best postponed or avoided. If a person changes their mind during sexual activity, then sexual activity should also change or stop. Sometimes the mind is willing but the body does not want to cooperate. In any event, people in a sexual encounter need to pay attention to each other, and to any shifts in attitude about or enthusiasm for the encounter that they might have.

People are willing to engage in consensual sexual relations for many reasons. Some may do so in exchange for money, as in prostitution. Others need (or desire) security and/or status, and enter into a relationship or marriage based on the exchange of sex for other goods. Other reasons for consensual sex include the need or desire to return a favor, such as an expensive meal or a vacation trip, or the desire to reduce sexual tension, or the willingness to appease a partner's sexual desire (as in a "quickie"—a brief, friendly, and release-accomplishing sex act, where only one person's orgasm is sought as an end), or the desire to share affection or express love, or the desire to have children, etc.

Regarding the contexts of friendship, love, and marriage, it is worth noting that consensual sex is not simply (or only) "consensual sex between strangers," but also "sex when there is willingness (of both members of a couple) to have sex." In other words, we would expect sexual contexts such as friendship and love to include consent (because people wouldn't force sex on someone they like or love). Because marriage can be reduced to a contract and does not technically require liking or loving one's spouse, it is not bound, by definition, to sexual consent.

Then there is also sex for pleasure's sake—sex for physical enjoyment, but without love or perhaps even without friendship or liking. When sex is primarily recreational, special care should be taken. In the Don/ Donna Juan case, for example, both consent and pleasure may exist, but encounters still rank fairly low in care across the range of possible intimate human relations. When having sex for sport, being honest about relational status ("this is just for fun, and not the start of a relationship"), attending to contraception, and taking measures to prevent the spread of STDs are just a few of the ways people need to protect themselves and others from negative fallout from sexual relations, and this may be less likely when partners' levels of care and concern for themselves and/or each other is low.

When it comes to consensual sex, the better situations are when the willingness to have sex is clearly expressed and meant, and when the willingness to have sex is the least bound by trade or (a sense of) obligation. When in doubt about these situations, other, less sexually intimate practices—or no sexual activity at all—may be wise.

# Liking

Sharing affection is another ethic of sex. In the liking ethic, sexual intimacy is seen as a potentially meaningful communicative act, or as a social act with potentially meaningful communicative implications. Intimacies express feelings, and offer the kinds of closeness and bonding that a purely thinking and talking (or telephoning, emailing or Facebooking) person would not be able to achieve. This is because human alienation, a psychological state, is not simply the result of psychological forces. The body is a profound part of the story. The body is also part of most stories that would undermine alienation. Just as kisses of greeting, high fives, hugs, friendly shoves, and gentle caresses are part of the human vocabulary of affection, so too are sexual intimacies. In the larger set of interpersonal and social interactions (including all forms of communication), the psychological pleasure of embodied sexual intimacy can be an important paradigm case and grounding force.

Sometimes a friendship can turn into a love or marital relationship, but sex would not suffice as the only factor inspiring a shift in ethics. At other times, a friendship can offer a safe context for sexual experimentation. Some people seek out a friend for their first sexual experience. Others may want to have sex but may not be in love, or they may not feel the need to associate sex with love, or they may have hope for finding love in the future but want to have some sexual experiences beforehand (or anyway). Others may have a "bed buddy," for whom they have at least some affection as a means to physical pleasure and comfort.

While some psychological pleasures of sex are satisfying, others can be dangerous. It is easy for people to turn to sex and sex relations to compensate for other things lacking in their lives. When warm embraces or kind words or care are wanted, but exist only as a prelude to less-desired sexual relations, the ethics of sex may be questionable. Consent in this instance is present, but only at a threshold level, and obligation and confusion muddy the encounter. When power and talent in the world are desired, but exist only through the racking up of multiple sexual relations, or a reputation for bringing sexual pleasure to others who have power or fame (such as rock-star groupies), or sexually manipulating others who have power or fame (e.g., political paramours), the ethics of sex may also be questionable.

In any event, when psychological pleasure operates independent of other important values of sex and sexual practice, interactions and intimacies may be ethically suspect.

## Love

For humans, emotional bonding is often given as one of the most significant reasons—if not *the* most significant reason—for having sex (and for wanting to have sex). This bonding can range from liking and affection, to deep and profound feelings of love. Attitudes about the importance of different kinds of affection and/or love vary from person to person and culture to culture. Much depends on the relative value given to certain kinds of love relations as a quality and practice in human experience, notions of "the individual" and ideas about how love fits into individual growth and maturation, and the kinds of intimate/love relationships experienced or witnessed by a person.

One challenge in talking or writing about love is the word "love" itself. The English language is not particularly strong in its words for emotions, relation states, and relationships, and has only one word for love. In ancient Greece, there were many words for love, but this doesn't necessarily help matters. The Greeks regularly used terms like *philia*, *agape*, and *eros* interchangeably, and variations in context make translating the meaning of these terms difficult.[5] Nevertheless, the Greeks frequently used the word "eros" to identify the kind of love ranging from the lustful "zeal of organs for one another" to love directed to or exclusive to one other person, a "private" kind of love, often erotic or sexual (or having been at some point erotic or sexual). In English, some people use "romantic love" to mean eros, but the terms "romance" and "romantic" come from a different historical moment, and are frequently associated with young people, early stages of love relationships, unrequited love, and/or love of the eyes (only). These are not limitations I wish to imply. In the next few paragraphs, then, I use the terms love or eros, depending on the situation, and hope that the context of the sentence gives enough guidance for proper interpretation.

Serious emotional and sexual bonding often involves exclusivity (monogamy or marriage) and a substantial amount of time. Sometimes eros is associated with luxury, as it may require the absence of poverty, and at least basic physical, material, and emotional security.[6] Sometimes eros is associated with luck, as in finding a compatible partner or one's "soul mate." In any event, eros can give other values of sex—physical pleasure, psychological pleasure, monogamy, and marriage, for example—fuller context and fuller meaning.

Sex and sex relations help weave lovers together interpersonally into a coherent and resilient unit. This is especially impressive in a world where self-sufficiency, individual rights, self-determination, ownership, and going it alone are valorized, often at the expense of others or the social fabric. By means of sex, lovers share themselves profoundly with each other, and may even briefly escape the mundane and burdensome details of existence. Emotional bonding, particularly eros, is what makes human sex more than simply an animal practice. For many, the emotional bonding of love is what makes human sexuality proper, unique, special, and complete.[7]

At first glance, the sex ethic of love may seem like a more liberal ethic than the ethic of marriage, because it does not require that a couple be married in order to have sex. But the ethic of love is actually more conservative than the marriage ethic.[8] Unlike a contract that legally sanctions sex practices at any time or for any reason between married partners, love demands people honestly take stock of their feelings (and not pursue sexual intimacy if love, or liking, or consent is not present), take personal responsibility for the welfare of others, be aware of each situation as it presents itself, and be attentive to thoughts and feelings at every moment.

Difficulties with emotional bonding and eros arise at times when relationships and affections begin and end, where affections are unclear in individuals, or are out of balance in couples, where circumstances external to relationships are challenging, and where problems of pleasure (or lack of it) persist. Because power and control are valorized in many cultures, people can fear becoming vulnerable to others, and can be afraid to love. The openness needed for emotional intimacy requires a kind of bravery seldom celebrated in popular culture, and seldom rewarded in everyday life. Instead of practicing this bravery, many people look for someone who will give *them* love, shopping for the perfect mate, as if that mate were a car, a box of cornflakes, or some other consumer product.[9] Others fall in and out of love so quickly that the reality or weight of their affections are suspect.[10] In some cases, people think they're in love when what they are feeling is only their sense of relief at finding ANY person to be with in a relationship (and this feeling is enhanced when past loneliness has been substantial).[11] In other cases, affections are out of balance or grow out of balance, or the world gets in the way, or love is present but barriers to pleasure leave one or both participants consistently physically unsatisfied. All these things can result in distraction, confusion, and other emotional, relational, and/or sexual problems.

Eros sometimes suggests the appropriateness of marriage. However, not all people who love each other want to marry, should be married, or perhaps are in a position to be married. Another response to eros is serial monogamy—the practice of having successive sexually exclusive partnerships, but having potentially more than one of these partnerships over time. Serial monogamy would not be defined as a series of one-night stands, because sexual exclusivity suggests more than one sexual encounter with the same partner, but there are more (and less) flattering versions of the practice. In its less flattering form, serial monogamy involves people who are faithful, but who fall in and out of love (or liking) quite frequently. In its more flattering form, serial monogamy describes people who make a commitment to one partner at a time (in marriage or otherwise, to a partner who they love or like), and who, if it came to it, would choose to break up that relationship rather than cheat. Serial monogamy without marriage offers some of the benefits of marriage (the promise of commitment and exclusivity, emotional security, etc.) but not all of them (social recognition, legal rights and protections, employee and insurance benefits, the finality of "until death do us part," tax breaks, a public and contractual commitment to the support and practice of child rearing, etc.).

To decide if marriage is right, love between partners is desirable, and some would say love is ethically required. Other factors (financial situation, career goals, pregnancy or existing children, desire for children, etc.) may also play into the decision to marry. Being sure about love is not simple, but when in doubt, it is unwise to rush. Having to ask "Am I in love?" may be one indication love is not present. In general, honesty in thought and discussion about these matters is helpful, and so is patience.

Because today's ideology of marriage is closely associated with love, the absence of love or the loss of love suggests it may be right to dissolve a marriage. However, not all married people (or serial monogamists, for that matter) should split up just because love has temporarily faded or even permanently dissolved. External forces may be partly to blame (for instance, occupational stresses, care-giving stresses, financial challenges, health problems), and some of these forces can change or be influenced to the extent that love will resurface. In other cases, severe injury or illness (e.g., brain damage, Alzheimer's disease) may reduce or eliminate a person's capacity for love and affection. Still, the love and strength of one person may be enough to sustain the relationship. One variable that must be seriously considered when eros wanes and a breakup is considered is the well-being, security, and material and emotional support of any children involved. Because children are more physically, psychologically, and emotionally vulnerable than adults, love and care for them must be a top concern.

## Marriage

Sexual intimacies are often justified by pointing to the fact that the people engaged in them are married. Marriage was at first a tribal and religious practice, and later also became a practice sanctioned by nation-states.[12] Marriage binds men and women together to ensure economic survival, enhance social standing, continue family lines, and provide for the care of children. Marriages used to be arranged, for the most part, by families and communities. Today, however, arranged marriages in the United States are rare. Some arranged marriages can be found in immigrant groups retaining the traditions of their home countries, polygamous religious minorities, cults, the upper classes, and reality TV shows, but for the last hundred years or so, companionate marriages—marriages where partners are lovers, friends, pals, economic partners, and parents all in one—have been depicted in books, magazines, radio, television, and advertising as the ideal.

Sex is socially sanctioned by marriage, but this does not by itself solve all sexual problems, or make sex "right" in all instances. Some states in this country, for example, have marital rape laws recognizing the unethical nature of forced sex between married people. Because marriage does not require love or even liking, it cannot provide adequate ethical direction in many sexual situations. Even when married people like or love each other, instances may arise where the right thing to do sexually is not made clearer by the fact of marriage alone.

Waiting until marriage to have sex has often been a good idea, especially for women who do not have access to reliable contraceptives, and/or who live in patriarchal cultures where female sexuality is tightly controlled. In some cases, waiting until marriage to have sex is a religious or subcultural mandate. It may also be a way to focus on other pursuits, avoid disease, and/or gain and retain social status (as in the case of cultures where virgins are considered more marriageable).

In the United States today, however, waiting until marriage to have sex is made more difficult by the increasingly rapid onset of puberty, as well as technologies, such as the birth control pill and condoms, that mitigate the risks of sex. Complicating matters is the challenge of self-sufficiency. Years of schooling, difficulties finding steady and fulfilling work, and the personal and social fragmentation that comes from the complexities of a high-tech global marketplace mean it takes people longer to support themselves, develop a sense of self, and establish a place (or places) in the world. When sexual maturity and social maturity do not coincide, problems can arise. In some instances, people marry early to fit with cultural or religious expectations, only to divorce after one or both members of the couple change in some significant way, or lose interest in the relationship. The demands of career, material success, fame, and consumer culture also can undermine marriage, as can popular—and perhaps inordinately high—expectations of companionate marriage, especially during the child-rearing years. In some cases, this can lead to frustration or infidelity. While none of this is new, much of it is aggravated by the current social, cultural, and economic climate.

Despite temptation, ethical marriage requires fidelity. (Here I exclude "open marriages," which are beyond the scope of this discussion.) It is wrong for married people to be sexually intimate with anyone other than their partners (or in the case of polygamy, with anyone outside of the marital unit), because in doing so, a major promise is broken (additionally, partners are potentially exposed to physical and emotional harm). If a person is unmarried, but has promised a partner that he or she will be monogamous, sexual intimacy outside the relationship would likewise be wrong. It would also be wrong for a person to be sexually intimate with someone whom they know to be otherwise committed or married. In all these instances, a profound trust is broken. While this behavior may be explainable, and even sometimes forgivable, it is unethical, regardless of arguments about mitigating circumstances.

## Making a Baby

Sometimes people have sex because they are trying to have a baby. While pregnancy is most often the unintended result of sex (the sex having been engaged in and justified by ethics already mentioned), in some cases, people have sex intentionally or perhaps primarily to become pregnant. This is especially true now that contraception has made non-procreative sex more of an expectation or norm (and procreative sex, therefore, more of a choice). In these instances, individuals or couples may consciously have sex to make a baby and skip the protections they might otherwise use, or try to time their sexual activities (intercourse) to ovulation cycles. In addition, women who want to get pregnant, but who are not particularly interested in sexual intimacy, (hetero)sexual relations and/or a relationship with their baby's father, may foreground conception, and leave other interpersonal matters by the wayside. In some cases where pregnancy is desired, but not a sexual relationship, or when conception is desired but is unsuccessful, efforts to have children may include other measures that move prospective mothers or parents into realms beyond interpersonal sexual intimacy (such as sperm banks, in vitro fertilization, surrogate motherhood, fertility treatments, adoption, and so forth).

Sex engaged in for the purpose of making a baby is related to individual, social, and transcendent meanings and needs that relate to children, childbearing, or child rearing. This does not deny such meanings for "surprise pregnancy" sex (sex resulting in an unplanned, but welcomed, pregnancy); however, if these meanings are attributed to "surprise pregnancy" sex, they are attributed *after* the fact of the sex (and are not part of the rationale for sex before or during sexual activity).

On an individual level, procreation offers the ego gratification of offspring who share a family resemblance, traits, and talents. Procreation also leads to uniquely extensive and intimate nurturing opportunities. Interpersonally, having children may result in the bonding and growth that comes from a shared cause and sharing the status of "parent" to a child. Being a parent also opens up new social relationships with other parents, and may deepen familial relationships, both within and across generations. On a transcendent level, children provide a means of linking to the cosmos and taking part in one of the great mysteries of life. Having children also helps satisfy the human fear of death and our desire for immortality, though the outcome of this is not always good.[13] It has been argued, for instance, that the fear of death and the desire for eternal life, combined with the discovery of paternity, led to patriarchy—the history of men controlling women and women's sexuality to ensure lineage.[14] There is also the problem of parents who try to live their lives again—vicariously—through the lives of their children, pushing their children (regardless of the children's own interests) toward things they, the parents, wished they'd done, or excellences they never achieved.[15]

From a biological perspective, sexual reproduction is not only required for the continuation of the species, it is *good* for the continuation of the species. Sexual reproduction is preferable to asexual means of reproduction (e.g., cloning—as practiced by viruses, bacteria, some invertebrates, etc.—as well as by scientists in the laboratory), because sexual reproduction involves the shuffling of genetic material. Since offspring are not carbon copies of their parents, they are more likely to survive in fickle environments. Diversity of offspring means that as environments change over time and across territories, at least some offspring will "fit" with new situations and survive to breed again.[16]

Biologists measure the "success" of a particular organism or species by the quantity of its progeny and the genetic material that its progeny embody and carry forward to the next generation. Human success is measured in more ways than this, but there is still a fascination with men and women who have numerous offspring; eugenics is not a completely dead science, and concerns about the diminution of the "white race," etc., persist. Few people use survival of the species as a rationale for sexual intimacy, though some people may feel pressured to do what others around them do and have children, or feel pressure to give their parents grandchildren, or feel pressure to keep their particular … genetic, familial, or "racial" line alive or pure.

Having sex in order to make a baby is related to a wide variety of needs and meanings beyond the communicative and interpersonal needs and meanings with which this book is most concerned. But such sex is still an important part of the story of sexuality and sex ethics.

# The Sex Ethics Diagram

People have sex for different reasons. When a person tries to justify why they are being sexually intimate with another other person, they usually give at least one of six explanations as to why it's OK, or good, or right.[17] These six rationales for or "ethics" of sex were discussed in the last chapter, and are listed below:

- It feels good
- The other person consents to it
- I like the person
- I love the person
- I'm married to the person
- I'm/we're trying to make a baby

These six ethics of sex may operate independently, or in combination with each other. Often, one ethic alone is not enough (for the civilized and humane person). Having sex because it feels good physically does not eliminate rape or necrophilia (sex with the dead) as a practice. Having sex with someone who consents could include exploitative forms of prostitution, or fake, gold-digging marriages, neither of which are attractive sorts of relations. Generally, people want sexual encounters that include feeling good and consent, and many people want to be married to, or love, or at least like their sexual partner(s).

In any sexual event, it's important for people to be clear about what they're doing, and why they're doing it. Getting drunk or otherwise chemically altered and dumping responsibility is a popular tactic, but it doesn't play out well in the end for either sex, emotionally or practically. It especially doesn't play out well for women, who have somewhat more to lose than men when engaging in sexual intimacy (in terms of potential sexually transmitted diseases and possible pregnancy). It is also important for people to be clear with others about what it is they think makes sex with those others right, good, or OK. Is this sex for sport and "we're both just having fun"? Is this part of a love relationship? Is this simply mutual consent? Am I just using this person as a sperm donor? And so on. It's not that if you don't want your expectations violated or your feelings hurt or your heart broken, then you shouldn't violate other people's expectations or hurt their feelings or break their hearts. It's that doing these things to other people is unloving, and therefore, unethical.

If we put the sex ethics into a diagram, this is what we see:

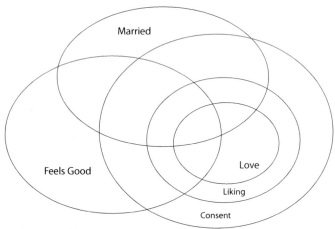

The V. V. Peterson Sex Ethics Diagram

The one ethic of sex that does not appear in the diagram is "I'm/ we're trying to make a baby." This rationale for sex is not included in the diagram, because it differs in kind from the others. Specifically, and as mentioned earlier, procreative motives are caught up in a whole different set of meanings and needs, which may include ego gratification, the desire to nurture children, a way to link to the cosmos, the desire for immortality, and so on. Because of this, the "I'm/we're trying to make a baby" ethic could be located anywhere in the diagram: in any part of any of the ovals (a husband and wife getting pregnant, a woman using a friend as a sperm donor), or in its most depraved form, as its own completely separate oval. It can be written into the diagram as a note accompanying any X's marking a spot, if and where making a baby is also a goal.

Love and liking are nested ovals, because they are similar in kind. "Liking" has the potential to condense or transform into "love," or it may be its own thing, as between friends who may think of sex as a pro-social act. Because love is rarer (a taller order) than "liking," it is a subset of that broader ethic. Both the love and liking ethics have been placed inside the consent oval, because if you like or love someone, it would be unethical to have sex with that person without that person's consent.

The other two ovals are "feels good" and "married." The spaces that result within and between the ovals describe the place a person might be in any sexual encounter: In love, feeling good, but not married; or married and feeling good; or liking someone, but not married and the sex not feeling good, etc. There is *no significance* to the relative size of each part of the oval. The diagram, like all other Venn diagrams, does not address or reflect proportion.

Can you locate yourself and your own practices in the diagram? Are you not even on the diagram? This would be true if you don't have a sexual partner right now. Perhaps you are satisfying some of your sexual needs by yourself and for yourself. This can be a good thing, and not only because for men it may help to stave off prostate cancer. To quote Phil Hartman from a *Saturday Night Live* skit, "When you're a one-man [or one-woman] band, nobody gets hurt."

Are you in the smallest upward pointing triangle—married, in love, feeling good during sex, and maybe even trying to have a baby? Or are you in some other space? A Catholic friend of mine who used birth control and lived with her boyfriend for years before they were married and before they decided to conceive said she had this kind of guilt-free, "ideal" sex three times in her life (three attempts at pregnancy, then illness precluding intimacy, then back to using birth control). Was the rest of her sexual life unethical? The answer is not as simple as orthodoxies suggest.

Social, cultural, and religious ideals of sexuality are difficult to reach, occasionally ambiguous or contradictory, and may not always be desirable when viewed from other viable perspectives. Mandates about sex for procreation only, or characterizations of married sex as a means of containing the ugly practice of fornication, for example, ignore and undermine the social and humanizing aspects of sex and sexual intimacy.[18] And abstinence is a very good idea at some times in a person's life, but would end the species if it were practiced universally. In response, it may be tempting to throw the responsibility "baby" out with the ideals "bathwater." But extreme relativism (or outright sexual barbarism), is also a poor way to proceed. In addition to sexual ideals, we need sex ethics.

So you may want to ask yourself, "Where am I in the sex ethics diagram?" Are you having sex with barely any consent? Does sex feel good—or does it feel like a duty? Are you really in love? Are you doing what you can to make sex pleasurable for your spouse/lover/partner/friend/pickup? Are you waiting to have sex until you're married? Are you in the friend zone, or the one-night stand mind-set, and are you being honest about that with the other person (or persons) about that mind-set? Are you using adequate precautions against unwanted pregnancy and disease? How can you be more ethically responsible to your sexual partner(s)? How might you be more ethically responsible to yourself?

# Vulnerability

Human beings are all vulnerable—embodied, biological, and mortal beings—although we may not want to admit it. Because we have bodies like other animals, we need to eat and eliminate waste. We are subject to physical harm from without, and physical pain and suffering from within. Suffocation, drowning, starvation, and other deprivations can make us suffer and cause us death. Environmental dangers such as toxins, forces of nature, accidents, illnesses, enemy others, extremes of heat and cold, and other hazards should remind us that our fates are not solely held in our own hands.

But we often forget about the fact that we are vulnerable. When we are satiated (with food, drink, sleep, sex, etc.), "under control" and without pain, and when our words and actions come easily, our bodies are, for the most part, transparent to us—like panes of glass that we fail to acknowledge as part of a window. But when we are deprived of satisfaction, or when we feel pain or disability or disintegration, the body seems to leap out of its unity with the mind, attracting our attention, and forcing us to deal with it as a separate "thing."[19]

To complicate matters, humans are a special kind of animal, one whose vulnerability extends beyond issues of simple physical survival of organism and species.[20] Because we humans use symbols and create realities all our own (both shared and individualized), we respond to more than just the physical world of "what is there." Humans have deep memory, and also can imagine "what might be," and these capacities launch us into a whole new world of both possibility and vulnerability.[21] This means that "things," for us, are more than simple objects of perception; they are colored by past events and future hopes. This also means that we are not just organisms, but "selves" who develop—selves with complex emotions wrapped up in concerns about image and normalcy and wholeness and individuality. Humans can imagine how they might someday be different from how they are now, and can imagine and be concerned with what other humans might think.[22] This forecasting capacity means that symbol use and other signs can themselves be experienced viscerally. Not only do sticks and stones break bones, but words and actions can hurt as well. It is no wonder so many expressions we have regarding relationship and communication are derived from metaphors that foreground the physical realm, and highlight physical pleasure and pain (for instance, what she said was a "shot to the heart," he's a "pain in the neck," she's a "breath of fresh air").

The physical and emotional vulnerabilities mentioned above are shared by all humans, but just because all bodies share *many* qualities of vulnerability doesn't mean that all bodies share *all* qualities of vulnerability. Young and old bodies, able and disabled bodies, and male and female bodies differ in important ways. Such differences can lead to confusion and problems, especially when one form of body is taken as the standard or ideal for a particular context, and when "other" bodies are compared against that ideal body and are found lacking.[23] This is just as likely as, say, when men are taken as the typical body in medicine and surgery (where prostheses and drug dosages don't "fit") as it is when women are taken as the typical body in child care (where fathers find it hard to change their baby's diaper when changing tables are located in "women-only" public spaces).

What follows is an effort to clarify different vulnerabilities in male and female bodies while affirming the shared vulnerability of all people (and while avoiding a reduction of the sexes to "essences").[24] I discuss mainly physical differences, because these are the most straightforward differences between men and women, and because some of the more generic emotional or psychological vulnerabilities characteristic of each sex are at least partly grounded in these differences. I only suggest some of the implications of these differences here, since the significance of these differences can only be judged by each individual in his or her own particular culture, and in each particular situation.

The first vulnerability has to do with relative body size. There is a vulnerability that comes with being a smaller (and weaker) person rather than a larger (and stronger) person. Children are most vulnerable in this way, and women often are as well. Particular instances do not always fit the statistics, but adult women are often smaller and weaker than the adult men with whom they interact. This difference in size between men and women is made even more likely by cultural expectations (where the ideal relative size of males and females in heterosexual couples in the United States is "male slightly taller than female").[25] This means that in most two-person settings, with one man and one woman, the woman could be more easily overpowered by the man than vice versa (and a child could be more easily overpowered by either adult). Being overpowered can include rape, battery, coercion, and other forms of abuse that physical size may allow.

When people lack size as a way to enforce their opinions or desires, they may resort to other means of power such as bribery, seduction, intellect, money, trickery, reasoning, etc. Of course, brute force is often discouraged as uncivil, so larger people are expected to avoid its use. Still, some men bully and intimidate women and children. Women also bully and intimidate children. For some, this can be the primary form of discipline. Past abuses and the emotional scars left by such forceful manipulations can be deeply felt and difficult to forget. If not consciously rejected, they may also set the tone for future actions.

Vulnerabilities of women are also related to fecundity and menstrual cycles. From an early age, young girls must get used to a monthly phenomenon where a bloody substance comes out of their reproductive organs. Unlike other mammals, the human menstrual flow is especially heavy and debilitating (e.g., most women become iron deficient during their period and experience pain). It requires some form of attention (changes in activities, wearing of absorbent materials) and sometimes interferes with the performance of everyday tasks, as well as specialized jobs.

Menstruation may be handled better or worse by particular women, depending on the intensity of the period itself, access to hygiene products, and access to and use of drugs or medicines that may limit the severity or occurrence of symptoms. Also relevant is the way menstruation is given meaning by the culture, friends, family, religion, and other institutional and circumstantial forces (in other words, is it seen as a rite of passage into womanhood, a "curse," an annoying disability requiring sick leave?). But regardless of whether menstruation is greeted with celebration, resignation, fear, consternation, or a shrug of the shoulders, the experience of not being able to control a fluid emanating from one's body mimics incontinence, and this is easily perceived as a loss of bodily control. Menstrual blood looks something like "regular" blood, so getting used to seeing and dealing with it may help women deal with their own and others' future injury, illness-related pain, bodily excretions, and even death. This may partly explain why women often handle the sight of blood, physical pain, medical treatment, hospitals, and funeral homes better than men.

The ability to have a baby is a form of power, especially when there is a desire for procreation, and material and social support for it. Throughout history, this form of female power has been worshipped, coveted, feared, appropriated, and mimicked by men and male-dominated cultures (see, for example, the way Athena, the ancient Greek goddess of war, was said to have been "born" from the head (or thigh) of Zeus, and how monks of the early Christian church regularly used terminology of propagation and birth in their religious writings).[26] But the ability to have a baby also means that if the desire to conceive a child does not exist, or if social support or resources do not exist, then fertile women are at social and personal risk when they engage in potentially procreative sexual intimacies. This is why contraception, in many sexual relations, is an ethical necessity. It also means that women who are concerned with their own social welfare (and who do not have or use birth control and are not in a situation conducive to child rearing) are more likely to take a "defensive" stance when it comes to sexual intimacies, especially those that may lead to pregnancy.

Rape is another territory of vulnerability. The physical design of women means that they have more than one way of being raped, but men (and smaller men and male children especially) are not exempt from this form of violence. When trying to make sense of rape, much depends on the culture, friends, family, religion, etc., and how these individuals and groups participate in making sense of forced sex and the physical act of bodily penetration. In many cultures, rape is an extremely concrete means of asserting the vulnerability of another person—or kind of person, as in the case of raping the women on the losing side of a battle, or when men choose prostitutes or some other class of person as their victims, or in cultures where the rape of women is not seen as a crime, because the status of women is so low. In the United States, women enjoy a relatively high social status, and rape is considered a serious crime. But because our notions of masculinity do not mix well with vulnerability, male rape victims are less likely to tell others if they have been raped and less likely to get help with the emotional fallout of their experience. Women have the added vulnerability, however, of possible impregnation by a rapist, and this presents a whole new set of challenges.

Other vulnerabilities of humans are related to hormones. Variations in hormone production are common, and many are beyond a person's control (although pharmaceutical drugs have somewhat altered this fact). Occasional extremes are also typical, some of which have developmental, health, and even aesthetic implications. Both women and men experience fluctuations in their hormone levels, and this can lead to variations in their sense of strength, energy, attractiveness, sharpness or dullness of mind, and foci of attention.

The hormone testosterone, more prevalent in men but significant to both sexes, is related to maturation of secondary sex characteristics, muscle mass, bone strength, libido, and other matters. If levels are low, physical and/or emotional problems may result. In women, higher levels of estrogen and progesterone are related to menstruation, pregnancy, and nursing, and can also affect women's behavior in important ways. For example, hormones can help women bond with the children they breast-feed. Hormones of menstruating or premenstrual women often render them more sensitive to their surroundings, which can be seen as a problem of skewed perception, or as a temporarily heightened insight into social relations.

Significant shifts in hormones occur across the human life span. Puberty and menopause are two of the more prominent developmental milestones, but other significant shifts may also present themselves, depending on the individual. Whether a person's hormones vary more across the month or the day or the life span, it is important to recognize how we, as humans, are partly our hormones.

Vulnerabilities unique to men frequently derive from their sex organs. Unlike a woman's sexual equipment, a man's private parts are exposed and especially sensitive to injury. It is true that soft tissues of women are also rather exposed and may be harmed during physical activity, but not to the extent of a man's. One has only to watch a typical football or soccer game to see how, even with the best protective gear, the tallest and strongest man can be brought down by a blow to the groin (which is why self-defense classes spend a good deal of time focusing on this area). While this vulnerability may be downplayed, its significance is suggested by compensatory measures that either highlight the permanence and sexual/reproductive power of the male organ, or denigrate the potency or power of females. For example, in ancient Greece, Herm statues were featured all around the city of Athens. These marble sculptures were busts set atop posts, and the post featured no other human feature but a permanently erect penis.[27] Other cultures have created their own penis totems (sculptures, fancy cars, phallic architecture), and in this country, a weak or "wimpy" man is called a "pussy" (slang for female sex organs), while the epithet "dick" is reserved for the more actively offensive sort of male.

Like menstruation, the male sex organs may also participate in unexpected and uncontrolled flow, as in the case of nocturnal emission (wet dreams). This kind of flow also can be seen as embarrassing, and/or as a "rite of passage" into adulthood. Its relative infrequency, brief appearance during the male life span, association with pleasant dreams rather than painful cramps, and the less intimidating nature of the fluids involved, may make the occurrence a bit less challenging of an experience than menstruation. But it also serves as a reminder that some bodily things are not always under conscious control.[28]

Continuing along these lines, we may consider the erection. Unlike women's arousal, which may be more easily hidden or faked, men's sexual arousal, when translated into an erection, is more obvious. There is also the matter of performance in sexual intercourse, which is related to the relative size of private parts. Here, if there are problems with fit, blame is often laid on men (who are accused of being "too large" or "too small"). This is probably because men's organs are more visible than women's (and ignores the fact that women's bodies also vary in terms of size and potential for accommodation).

Intercourse, as traditionally defined, also requires of men (more so than women) the readiness of organs. For women, a lubricant may substitute for fluids absent of arousal or until arousal is achieved, but men usually need at least some degree of an erection for their part of the equation. Intercourse may also recommend that a man be able to control his organ, an organ that is not always so good at taking orders. Age, experience, health, intoxicants, consequences of surgeries, medications, and state of mind can all factor into the equation.

The social vulnerability implied by erections plays out in numerous and varied ways across cultures. Concerns about size, lack of control, and sexual performance are often reflected in dirty jokes and comedy routines, while matters of the male's contribution to female sexual pleasure have been addressed by sacred texts, matchmakers, marriage therapists, sex therapists, sex manuals and self-help books. Pharmaceutical and other treatments for erectile dysfunction and penile enlargement are now used not only by legitimate patients, but also by more "average" consumers, and also by the young (and otherwise healthy) for sport. By making erections foolproof, drugs like Viagra®, Cialis®, and Levitra® have eliminated some of the fickleness of male body parts, and have undermined or alleviated this centuries-old territory of male vulnerability.[29]

The interesting thing about vulnerabilities of all kinds is that, in and of themselves, they are not simply good or bad things. This is one of the reasons why, for example, social scientists may never get to the bottom of the issue of condom use. When people feel vulnerable to pregnancy and/or STDs, they often use a condom. But condom use is not simply a matter of "compliance gaining" (of getting another person to do what you want them to do). Condom use (or lack of condom use) is also a matter of intimacy. Trusting someone to be free of disease when they say they are, and coming in contact with someone in a very intimate way, without a physical barrier between skin, is a not just a matter of public health—it's a matter of closeness, and of vulnerability. This is why despite so many warnings and fear appeals, many people still have sex without latex. The analysis here is not meant to condone unsafe sex, but to help explain why it occurs, and to suggest better ways in which condom use might be encouraged—ways that see condom use not as a form of self-defense, but as a way to be loving, by recognizing and caring about the vulnerabilities of others.[30]

Our shared and special vulnerabilities are the basis of humanism. They are what help us recognize our need for each other, and our indebtedness to each other. By trying to remove vulnerabilities from our bodies and our lives, we may be fooling ourselves about how much power and control we really have over ourselves, and we may undermine our potential toward fuller humanity—our ability to allow ourselves to be vulnerable to others. On the other hand, sometimes we benefit from trying to reduce our vulnerability, as is the case when people exercise or eat healthy foods as a way to reduce their vulnerability to disease, or when they take precautions during sex to prevent physical or emotional harm. This means we need to think carefully about vulnerability, how we deal with our own vulnerability, and how we deal with the vulnerabilities of others. Men and women are vulnerable in many of the same ways, by virtue of being human, and we are vulnerable in different ways as well. Knowing this, we can either exploit these vulnerabilities in pathetic and hostile maneuverings for power, or we can honor these vulnerabilities and let the way we negotiate them gradually and carefully lead us toward, rather than away from, intimacy.

# Comments About Categories

Categories such as "male" and "female," "man" and "woman," "masculine" and "feminine," "gay" and "straight," are part of the vocabulary of sex and sexuality (as are "sex" and "sexuality" themselves). Understanding these terms and how they are used is important. Often, "male" and "female" are understood as natural given categories, determined primarily by body parts and hormones, but things aren't always that simple.[31] The terms "man" and "woman" are also seen as fairly biologically straightforward—in some cases, just another way to say male and female (although they are often much more than this). These terms may also be used to indicate suggested behaviors and social roles (that is, a woman will eventually become a mother, a proper woman does not sit that way, real men don't cry, men like to watch sports, and so forth).

The terms "masculine" and "feminine" are often associated with (and are also often used to direct) the behaviors and social roles attached to "man" and "woman" (e.g., nurturing is a feminine quality, masculinity means being tough, etc.). This can lead to difficulties when real people do not fit the roles or expectations others expect of them.[32] In addition to being descriptive terms, masculine and feminine are also emotionally charged terms, so much so that often men do not want to be called feminine, and women do not want to be called masculine, even when they agree that the qualities associated with these terms appropriately describe their character (supportive and caring, tough and strong, and so on). Because of this, it can be helpful (and I try) to use less overtly rather than more overtly gendered and emotionally charged adjectives to describe character or behavior, so that the broadest spectrum of listeners or readers might see themselves potentially addressed in any particular scenario.

Terms of sexual orientation such as "gay" and "straight," "homosexual" and "heterosexual," "lesbian," and "queer," for instance, are used to categorize classes of persons by the sex of their chosen sex partner(s), sexual orientation, behaviors, and/or sexual group affiliation. Labeling sexual orientation may be done by the person him- or herself or by others, and for various personal, social, and/or political reasons. Often, sexual orientation is an unclear category, because human sexuality is itself a fluid and varied collection of practices, experiences, and affiliations.[33]

In this book and elsewhere, I use the words "sex," "intimacy," "sexual intimacy," and "sexual practice" at different times and for different reasons. In some cases, it helps to be strategically vague. In other cases, the motivation is political. The traditional and largely procreative definition of sex as beginning and ending with the male—beginning with his erection and ending with his sperm-implanting orgasm—is not the only way of understanding sex, though it will probably remain the dominant way of understanding sex so long as technologies do not (further) supplant conventional means of conception. In contrast to procreative understandings, social understandings of sex and sexual practice shift the boundaries of traditional sex, and make it less clear where and when sex begins or ends for different individuals.[34] When boundaries are unclear, I may use the term intimacy or sexual intimacy instead of sex, but no inferiority or superiority of these terms, or the practices they involve, is implied.

Because I am primarily concerned with the ethics of interpersonal sexual relations, and because many of the subjects discussed here would apply just as well to either homosexual or heterosexual sexual relations or relationships, I intend my use of the terms man and woman in the same way male and female are used, and with an appreciation for the complexities and overlap of what we call "the sexes."[35] In other words, I don't think of men and women or males and females as opposites (that is, men/males are more the "opposite" of geese than they are the opposite of women/females), and I try to avoid narrow sex/gender stereotypes when I can. I try to acknowledge that the sexes are not simply given, but are a complex of hormones, body parts, chromosomal structures, social experiences, and histories of sexuality that decide what a "sex" is, and how important it is to be one (the treatment of intersex babies is a good example of this).[36] I also try to avoid basing observations and arguments on sex research that measures and confirms self-evident, circular, and culturally predetermined gendered behaviors and roles. It's not that I deny differences between males and females, or men and women, or masculinity and femininity, or gay people and straight people. But I do not want to solidify differences that are less permanent or significant than some discussions of sex and sexuality would have people believe.

# Why Statistics Are Useless for Ethics

I t's not easy finding a way to talk about sexual ethics. The subject of sex is so charged with emotion and deeply ingrained preconceptions, that most people feel uncomfortable just bringing up the topic—even when they are experiencing serious problems. Sometimes, rules about sex are related to poorly justified or unjustifiable arguments. Religious mandates often fit this description, as do overextended claims emerging from psychological and sociological speculation about "liberated" practices. Such sources of advice about sex, whether "right-wing" or "left-liberal" often have their own agenda. Just the way sex is talked about by these sources (use of terms like "venal sin," "fornication," "sexual liberation" or "sexual freedom," for example) can oversimplify and predetermine what is sexually good or bad, right or wrong. To take a fresh and honest approach to the ethics of sex, these often deeply ingrained "understandings from on high" must be recognized and interrogated, so that if any of them are embraced, they are embraced out of reason and care, and not simply out of obedience and ignorance.

Turning to science doesn't always help matters. Scientific, social-scientific, and pseudoscientific research is not immune from the weight of precedent and human bias. As such, it often measures and confirms the gendered behaviors and roles that it expects to find.[37] Often, definitions of terms like "man," "woman," "masculine," "feminine," "normal," "satisfaction," "deviant," and "healthy" are circular and culturally predetermined. In other instances, terms are poorly defined, or shift their meanings across measures or within a study, or across a series of studies. Conditions under which studies are conducted and methods by which data are gathered and analyzed are frequently problematic, or are outright flawed. Questionnaires or interviews asking research subjects to report about past sexual practices are less likely to measure behavior and more likely to measure memory, and memory often fails, or is tinged by imagination and/or a desire to impress the interviewer or fit cultural expectations. On top of all this, laboratory settings are often bizarrely artificial; "failed" studies (studies discovering no differences) are seldom published; statistical findings are easily distorted; and real-life encounters are rarely analyzed (for obvious ethical reasons).[38]

In many instances, supposedly "objective" data about the sexes and sexual practices are shared as though they should have bearing on how people ought to act. This data is especially compelling to people in the United States, who are fascinated by numbers, polls, statistics, personality tests, and other seemingly "unbiased" measures. But we should not be so overly impressed by the findings of scientists or pseudoscientists that we overlook the biases of these human researchers, and the irrelevance of their findings to what is right.[39]

Psychology, sociology, and biology have not unlocked the secrets of human sexuality to reveal an essential or necessary sexual structure. Body parts, chromosomes, the brain, genes, hormones, lifetimes of experiences, and other factors all participate in shaping people's sex and sexuality. This does not deny certain facts (fertility, brain differences, hormonal differences, etc.). It simply asserts the complexity of humanity, the importance of interpretation, and the inability of facts to ever "speak for themselves."

In a democratic-minded culture that celebrates equality, where social climbing is possible and class demarcations are weak, and where a history of immigration has meant the successive assimilation of immigrant groups, the desire to fit in and "keep up with the Joneses" can be very strong.[40] People often think the safest thing to do is to know what everyone else does, and how everyone else does those things, and then do likewise. Simply "keeping in line" is seen as a virtue—even when care, concern, or forethought are absent about acts done.

But it is not a virtue just to do what everyone else does. For one thing, what everyone else does is often wrong. More importantly, the critical issue is not to try to discover what a "good practice" or a "bad practice" is, or how widespread a practice is, but to be able to decide *what practice is called for in a particular instance involving a particular person (or particular people).*[41] Knowing what is right to do can't be reduced to a formula, because each sexual situation is different. This is not only because each sexual situation suggests its own fitting response, but because people and cultures vary and change over time, so no one answer will fit all cases.

Knowing what is right to do cannot be left up to other people or authorities. We are not children forever. Eventually, most people face sexual situations for which there are no easy or ready-made answers. At that point, they have to make decisions for themselves, using their own ethical standards, what factual information they have at hand, and what they know of the culture, the situation, and the persons involved (including themselves).

## Endnotes

1. For more on differences between the senses, see Hans Jonas, 1979.
2. For more on the art of loving, see Erich Fromm, 1956.
3. John D'Emilio and Estelle B. Freedman, 1988.
4. For more on sex ethics, see Eugene Borowitz, 1969. The secular section of this book, *Choosing a Sex Ethic: A Jewish Inquiry*, is an inspiration to my entire book, and especially to this section of my book. Borowitz identifies and discusses four sex ethics: The ethics of healthy orgasm, consent, love, and marriage. I have given my own take on and updated these four areas of ethical concern, and added two more: liking, and making a baby.
5. A useful discussion of the complexities of etymology and the slicing and dicing of terms for love can be found in Robert C. Solomon, 1981, pp. 9–15.
6. For more on love as a luxury, see Erich Fromm, 1956.
7. Eugene Borowitz. 1969.
8. Eugene Borowitz, 1969.
9. For more on "shopping for a mate," see Erich Fromm, 1956.
10. Eugene Borowitz, 1969.
11. Erich Fromm, 1956.

12. Bertrand Russell, 1970.

13. Ernest Becker, 1973.

14. Leonard Shlain, 2003.

15. Jiddu Krishnamurti, 1953.

16. Joan Roughgarden, 2004.

17. One other rationale I did not include in the sex ethics list and sex ethics diagram is "for spiritual reasons." Modern-day Westerners seldom consider sex a form of prayer, or a means of glorifying God or communing with the spirit world, but in some religions and in some other cultures, sex may be understood in this way. People in the West, if they recognize such an ethic, probably subsume it under the "love" ethic—envisioning the loved one (and intimacy with the loved one) as a means by which a "higher" love may be attained or expressed (see, for example, Socrates' second speech on love in Plato's *Phaedrus*, 1956).

18. For more on this, see Baker and Elliston's discussion of Thomas Aquinas in their introduction to *Philosophy and Sex*, 1975.

19. Drew Leder, 1990.

20. Hans Jonas, 1979.

21. Leonard Shlain, 2003.

22. Josiah Royce, 1967.

23. Heidi Reeder, 1996.

24. For more on essences and essentialism, see Diana Fuss, 1989.

25. For more on gender norms and the hyper-ritualization of gender performance in advertisements, see Erving Goffman's *Gender Advertisements*, 1974.

26. David Noble, 1992.

27. For more on herms, see Martha Nussbaum, 1986.

28. For more on male flow, see Elizabeth Grosz, 1994.

29. Robert MacDougall, 2006.

30. Recent comments by Pope Benedict XVI regarding condom use are suggestive in this regard.

31. Judith Butler, 1993, and Michel Foucault, 1978.

32. Heidi Reeder, 1996.

33. See Jonathan Ned Katz's *The Invention of Heterosexuality*, 1996, and Adrienne Rich's discussion of the "lesbian continuum" in "Compulsory Heterosexuality and Lesbian Existence" in *Blood, Bread, and Poetry*, 1994.

34. Joan Roughgarden, 2004.

35. Heidi Reeder, 1996.

36. Joan Roughgarden, 2004.

37. Joan Roughgarden, 2004.

38. For more on weaknesses of sex/gender-related research, see Heidi Reeder, 1996; Catania, 1999.
39. Eugene Borowitz, 1969.
40. See William James, *Talks to Teachers*, 1958.
41. The ancient Greeks used the terms prepon (the right thing to do) and kairos (the right time to do something). For more on these terms, see John Poulakos and Takis Poulakos, 1999.

# Part II

## Communication

# Sex As Communication

Sexual intimacy is a complicated matter. It involves unique bodily configurations (every person's body is different), physiologically rooted drives and tastes, and socially and culturally shaped taboos, desires, turn-ons and turn-offs. Negotiating these territories is not easy, especially in the face of caricatures of sexual intimacy offered up by popular culture, and other sources of ideals of intimacy and identity (e.g., religion, sex manuals, experts, popular mythology). To address how sex and communication relate, we can break up the subject into two different, but overlapping, territories of concern: "sex as communication," which is a territory we share to some degree with other animals (and plants in some cases), and "communication about sex," which is a territory that is wholly human. The former is discussed next, and the latter is addressed in the following two chapters.

Sex is communication in the physiological sense—as a flower communicates its scent and its pollen, so too do intimate partners communicate aromas and tastes and sensations and substances. In the case of heterosexual sex as traditionally defined (and without barrier methods of contraception), fluids are communicated between participants in a way that may result in pregnancy. Other forms of sharing or mutual "contributing" of substances are also involved in intimate acts, as the rather unattractive slang expression for kissing "swapping spit" suggests. When we use the expression "*communi*cable diseases," we mean literally the sharing of fluids that harbor viruses, bacteria, etc., and that may harm health.

When we think of "communing" with nature, we may also be thinking of communication in this way. Although this more organic meaning of the term "communication" is not as common as it once was, it is worth noting that understandings of communication as speech, gesture, and performance are (at least metaphorically) related to this more biological, "sharing/contact/dispersal-oriented" sense of the term.

Sex is also communicative in an "indexical" sort of way. An indexical sign is a sign with a logical or causal connection to what it represents, as in "a robin is a sign of spring," or "a flushed face is a sign of sexual arousal."[1] The cause-effect connection between an indexical sign and the state or object it indicates is not foolproof (a flushed face may also indicate a fever or a menopausal hot flash), but indexes are still useful because they work sometimes and because we can get better at "reading" them over time, and use them to guide actions (e.g., When I did "x," "y" happened, so maybe "x" caused "y" and I should try/do "x" again). Indexical signs are often unintended by the person "sending" them (unconscious), and learning how to read a partner's indexical signs can be an asset in a sexual encounter.

Finally, sex is communication in a performing sense. Like the sequence of steps or movements made by a dancer when dancing, sexual vocalics and gestures are a form of nonverbal communication (which may or may not be supplemented by spoken utterances, and which may or may not be commented upon afterward). What a person performs—says or tries to say—in the intimate moment, with his or her body, nonverbal signals, movements, paralanguage, etc., may not always be clear when people are intimate, but meanings can, to some extent, be expressed, and are often inferred by both intended and unintended actions and movements. This means misunderstandings of performance can also occur. For example, does a movement away from a partner, while engaged in some intimate practice, mean "I don't want you to do that there now," or does it mean "I don't want you to do that there ever"? Does it mean "I'd like to stop doing this altogether," or does it mean "I'd like you to come pursue me"? Or does it merely mean "The button on the sofa is digging into my back so I need to move"? In some cases, further clarification with words may be needed. Nevertheless, sighs, cries, moans, and other nonword vocalizations; facial expressions, leanings, shifts of rhythm, lurches, shrugs, squeezes, and other such gestures and actions all count as possibly meaningful communicative aspects of performance.

# Communicating
# Interpersonally About Sex

M ost people think of successful sexual intimacy as involving not only their own sexual pleasure, but the sexual pleasure of a partner. From this perspective, some sort of communication (from simple expression to detailed direction) is an important part of sexual experience. It is important for people to be aware of—and honest about—their own likes and dislikes, and also to share what they know of those things, as well as matters of body, mind, and situation, with their intimate partners. It is also important to listen. Giving off body language and paying attention to a partner's body language is one way to convey and pick up on what is preferred, but sometimes a more direct and descriptive approach is needed. That is, sometimes people need to more explicitly *say* something, or use visual symbols that stand for words to convey something about what they like and don't like, how they feel, what they want, and even what's going on in their larger world, if they want to steer sexual activities toward desired actions and reactions.

In this way, humans are not like (other) animals. As self-reflexive creatures, we think not only in terms of "now," but in terms of our "selves," past actions, histories, meanings, and possible futures.[2] We communicate not only *with* our sexual actions, but *about* sex and sexuality. Intimate acts, expressions, and performances are not only potentially meaningful actions of the moment, they are also past actions subject to inquiry, and future possibilities subject to changes we might make or choose. When intimacy feels transparent, participants are not especially aware of themselves or their bodies or their "performance"; that is, they're not thinking too much *about* what's being done *in* the moment, they're just in the moment (what some people call "flow"). But in order for intimacy to feel or be transparent, some sort of common ground of meaning or understanding may be needed, and instances of happy transparent states will most likely require at least some communication about what is, has been, or will be going on.

Some people object to talking about sex. They think the best sex is sex without words—sex that needn't be talked about or include talk at all. This way of thinking is supported by myths, two of which relate directly to communication: "the myth of the mind-reading lover" (who understands a lover's need at every moment) and "the myth of the context-free sexual encounter" (for instance, no potential pregnancy, no sexual history to negotiate, no distracting cares of the world). These myths are pervasive in popular culture: We see them in TV shows, music, stories in popular magazines, Hollywood films, and pornography.

Life seldom mirrors these myths. This is not to deny the reality of sexual chemistry. Nor is it to deny the thrill that some people get from one-night stands. But the thrill of one-night stands may have as much or more to do with the taboos of behaviors engaged in, the satisfaction of pent-up desires, the thrill of conquest, and the temporary relief from not being alone, as it does with the quality of these temporary intimate encounters themselves. Ironically, feelings of liberation from social and cultural norms, fostered by temporary liaisons, and the "freedom of sexual speech" that can be experienced in such contexts, may make one-night-stand participants *more* inclined to communicate about their sexual needs than they would in more socially sanctioned relationships.[3] This may help explain the appeal of one-night stands for people who find sexual communication challenging, or whose conventional relationships suffer or have suffered from "communication breakdown," sexual or otherwise.

Nobody knows automatically what feels good to another person; what feels good to one person may not feel good to someone else. Heterosexuals face the added challenge of their partner having some body parts that are different from those with which they are more familiar (though it should be noted that having a same-sex partner does not remove the challenges of difference, "otherness," or unique and individual tastes). Because sexual intimacy can be rather complicated, rules of sex are often unhelpful. There are some things that we can say we know, in general, about men and women and pleasure, but these facts may have nothing to do with any individual person. And even when there is relative certainty about some sexual "fact," general knowledge is nothing until it is applied. This means that instead of searching for the "foolproof sexual technique" or "magic series of moves," people need to communicate before, during, and/or after sexual intimacy to fill in the gaps of understanding that science, sexual maxims, technique books, popular media, hearsay, and other sources of information will never fully address.

Early on, a person should probably try to find out how their sexual partner feels about *communication about* sex. For example, does the partner feel comfortable with talk (their own and/or the other person's) during sex? If so, can this talk take the form of direction, or should it be mostly sounds only, or words of encouragement? Is the partner willing to talk about sex afterward? Confidences may need to be built, and some verbal and nonverbal vocabularies established. Because of the sensitive nature of sexuality (e.g., its embodiment, its dangers, its significance to those involved), the *way* communication *about* sexual intimacy occurs is just as important as the information about sexual intimacy that is conveyed. Gentleness of tone, optimism and good humor, directness and clarity without crassness or hostility (including the careful use of terms and symbols), and a willingness to listen and respond to the concerns of others all help lead sexual partners toward what works and what is desired, not only early on in sexual intimacies, but across the span of intimate relations.

Fears of talking about sex are in some ways like fears of talking about a person's sense of humor. People don't want to talk about why they think a joke is or isn't funny because they fear it might ruin the pleasure of the joke, or future jokes. If we think of sexual intimacy as a "sense of humor," and if a person wants to enjoy "joking around" (sexual intimacy) with someone in the future, then it helps to know how particular kinds of jokes "work"—or don't—with that person (how intimate gestures are received by a partner), to get a feel for his or her sense of humor (sexual tastes). This critical analysis may take an occasional toll on a few particular jokes (sexual practices), at least until memory fades and the jokes can be told "fresh" again (and unlike jokes, welcome sexual techniques and practices take much longer to—or may never—get "old"). It would be unwise to spend too much time as a critic and not enough time as a jokester or appreciator—it's no fun if the joy of humor/sexuality is smothered by analysis. But discussing jokes would only undermine an entire sense of humor if there were only one joke to be had (only one way of doing intimacy), or if there were only one chance at getting a laugh (only one chance at sexual interaction), or if criticism was overdone or done poorly. In other words, discussing jokes doesn't necessarily undermine an entire sense of humor, and neither does discussing matters of sexual intimacy necessarily undermine sexual desire and the pleasures of intimacy. It is, however, a delicate matter.

One issue about which any sexual partner should feel entitled to comment is pain, and one word that should always be allowed during sex is "ouch."[4] Even though an expression indicating pain will likely be a turn-off to a partner, it is important that sex not become painful and one-sided. This is not simply because it is more likely that better sex (and thus perhaps *more* better sex) will happen in the future if things go well, but because it is important not to do harm to others. Sometimes there is a fine line between pleasure and pain, and in these instances it is not always clear what should be said or done. In general, however, a person knows when something hurts (or is becoming painful). In those instances, the person should say something, or clearly indicate as much, and their partner should respond in appropriate ways—that is, in ways that reduce or eliminate suffering. If pain distracts from a person's ability to become aroused or sustain arousal, or to act as a means to their partner's satisfaction, then it undermines intimacy. If there is something that could be done to alleviate the pain (e.g., a shift or change of position, use of a lubricant, lighter pressure/grip), this should be mentioned. In the long run, partners do each other no favor by bearing unpleasant sensations, nor is it good to ignore another person's discomfort. Such head-in-the-sand responses to pain can easily lead to resentment over past sexual encounters or trepidation regarding sexual encounters in the future, and this does little to promote intimacy and shared good feelings.

Another important focus of sexual communication is a partner's sexual tastes—a person's more predictable sexual likes and dislikes. Because sexual tastes are rooted in unique bodies, they are unique to individuals, but they also may be common to and shaped by cultures and social groups. Some sex and marriage manuals, for example, directly target particular social groups (for instance, gay, lesbian, Christian, Jewish, and so on), while broader cultural norms regarding sex and sexuality are conveyed in more diffuse and environmental ways. It is easier to have transparent sexual relations with someone if you share their sexual values, can read their intimate gestures, and enjoy the ways they communicate through touch and other verbal and nonverbal means. This doesn't require the complete sharing of sexual mores and tastes, or social group or culture, but it does point to the usefulness of exploring areas of shared sexual values, and catering (within reason) to the sexual tastes of intimate partners.

It is also worth mentioning that sexual tastes may vary, depending on the stage of arousal a person is in, and across a person's sexual life span. For instance, a man may become less sensitive to contact right after (first) orgasm, whereas contact that might be too intense to a woman at the outset of intimacy might be more welcome or desired at later stages of arousal.[5] Sexual tastes also may become more varied as a person becomes more sexually experienced. Pacing practices (teasing, variations of intensity, rhythm) are especially important in intimacy, because of the part they play in sexual momentum. These are all places where people need to be open to learning (and relearning) what works for themselves and for their partner(s).

Communicating about sexual likes and dislikes is important, especially when intimacy is new and unfamiliar, but it should be done in moderation. Too much talk during intimacy can be distracting and can undermine the flow of interaction (sex is no fun if the experience starts to feel like an experiment or exam). Too little direction during intimacy may make it hard for a partner to understand what is desired, because only in-the-moment direction could adequately convey such things clearly. In some cases, the coherence or momentum of a sexual encounter may have to be compromised, or even sacrificed, for the sake of communication that would benefit future encounters. In general, too much pre- or post-intimacy critical commentary about what is and isn't liked may curb enthusiasm for future interaction; not enough pre- or post-intimacy direction may leave a partner confused as to how to proceed next time. Humor is often an asset in sexual communication, but because taste is such a personal matter, humor about tastes should be used carefully and sparingly. As long as it is not seen as excessive or unseemly, positive commentary may be welcome.

Proper timing of commentary is also important. It helps to save constructive criticism for times that are close enough to an encounter for memory's sake, but far enough away in time from intimate acts that those acts can be considered while in a less physically and emotionally vulnerable state. Talking about sex a few hours or more after an encounter, for example, gives enough critical distance to speak about recent sexual activities while saving face. It also gives enough time to process the discussion and forget about the fact that matters were discussed, before the next encounter. If sexual partners are part of a relationship based on more than sex alone, they might remind themselves that they will have plenty of time to experiment and find things out about each other. If the relationship is mainly sexual and runs into sexual difficulties, it may be harder for the parties involved to take this long-term view.

Interpersonal semiotic systems (wholly invented signals and symbolic forms of communication) also may be used to communicate about bodies, needs, feelings, and the larger situation. These systems may be borrowed or original, simple or complex. Partners may agree, for example, to a few simple nonverbal cues, things like a twist of the torso or a squeeze of the hand on a shoulder. These cues would mean something that then would no longer need to be said verbally, during intimacy. For instance, a partner might say, "If I do this, … it means move up a little. … If I do this, … it means slow down a bit" or "when I move this way while you're doing this, it means I want you to ..." or "if I do 'X,' then that means I'd like you to lighten up pressure or your grip a bit." Because symbolic, signal-like kinds of semiotic communication are learned (and not causally related to their referent, as are indexical signs), they need to be explained explicitly (preferably outside the sex act itself) so that partners know the "message" of any signs used.[6]

Beyond simple gestural cues, other signs and signals such as code words, colors, music, theatrical and contextual cues, book excerpts and illustrations, etc., also may be invented and/or used to communicate about states of mind and body. For example, women may wear a particular style of underwear to indicate the "visit" of a menstrual cycle. Partners might come up with a secret code phrase to share their sexual desires with each other, even while in public (perhaps "we have some laundry to do tonight"). Or they may refer to books (e.g., I'd like to try what's pictured on p. 37). Or they may agree upon a conventional or unconventional nonverbal sign of sexual interest (maybe a particular lamp or candle being lit, the drapes or blinds being pulled, a particular kind of music being played). Perhaps they may make up their own name for a sexual position (e.g., let's 46). Maybe one or the other wears a particular garment to indicate sexual interest, and so forth.

When symbols are ambiguous (when they may or may not necessarily "mean" something), they may provide interpretive "wiggle room" in ways that help reduce the risk of losing face, ease disappointment, and enhance social and interpersonal harmony. Playing a particular kind of music, say, may or may not signify sexual interest, so if a partner does not respond in a sexual way, the music can appear to be chosen simply for its enjoyment value. The same might be said for an ambiguous caress. If a partner does not respond with sexual interest, the caress can be seen as simply an expression of affection. In any event, symbolic means of communication expand the sexual vocabulary into a wider nonverbal/visual territory. They also make it easier for bashful, "artsy," and more visually inclined people to steer sexual behavior in desired ways.

Other matters relevant to sex that also may require communication include situational factors (stresses, duties, chores, pressures), psychological concerns (taboos, fantasies, body image issues, fears, ideologies, etc.), and bodily matters (reactions to prescription or other drugs, the time of the month in a woman's menstrual cycle, the time of day, weight, health, contraceptive use issues, gastrointestinal matters, and bathroom needs, for example). All these things are intimately related to the way a particular sexual encounter will go (or if it will "go" at all). For instance, a sexual technique may need to be avoided if it is associated with a previous bad experience or taboo; a short break may be called for if contraceptive preparations are needed; a full stomach may preclude a position that would be just fine on an empty stomach; and a pot on a hot stove or kids nearing the end of their video entertainment may recommend a shorter, rather than longer, encounter.

The complexity of sexual practice recommends *against* thinking of sex as something a person can master once and for all, and *for* thinking of sex as a wide range of possible actions that may or may not be appropriate with any particular partner, in any particular intimate scenario and sequence of events. It also recommends that cultural myths or "facts" about male and female bodies, scientific findings, expert testimony about arousal, and ideas about bodies learned from any previous intimate partners may be worth considering, but may not necessarily be worth employing, especially when a partner's responses show that his or her arousal or desire operates otherwise. Unlike ways of thinking about sex that try to identify typical practices or "sure-fire" techniques (which can get boring over time), interpersonal ways of understanding intimacy highlight the need for interaction, attentiveness, and communication. They are more likely to leave room for variety, change, and the demands of particular individuals and situations.

# Communicating Publicly About Sex

## Metaphors and Narratives

C ommunication is also related to sex, in the ways understandings of sex and sexuality are shaped through public talk and public writing. This means that beyond sex as communication, and communicating interpersonally about sex, there is also the social practice of communicating about sex, and none of these contexts is wholly distinct or immune from the others. Consider the ways people talk about sex when they're with their close friends, in a locker room, at a late-night party, or gossiping on the phone. Or think about the way sex is depicted and discussed in popular magazines, novels, advertisements, TV shows, newspapers, sex manuals, and films. Think about how sex is defined by the pornography industry, with its conventions of visual and narrative form, and its generous helpings of exaggeration and fantasy. Whether the messages come from everyday conversation or the many varieties of popular culture, the way we talk about sex, is part of what makes sex what it is.

Often, ideas from popular culture take the lead in shaping our understandings about sex, with notions then trickling down into families and individuals. But plain old talk is also influential. In the everyday verbal give-and-take between family, friends, and others, people often aren't very direct about sex, because they see it as a private matter, and some people don't speak of sex at all (which is its own kind of statement). But despite reticence—and despite the fact that words often fall short—many people still use adjectives and metaphors and stories to describe their own sexual experiences or the real or imagined sexual experiences of others. And the result of this talk is no small matter.[7]

The way we describe things has a way of becoming concrete. In other words, the way we talk about things doesn't simply *describe* "things," *talk shapes and takes part in making or "realizing" the very "things" that exist for us.*[8] Without words for something, we might not even recognize "something" as a thing. This might not seem to be true of things like rocks or tables (as opposed to things like "trends" or "personalities"), because rocks and tables are things that we can gain access to and interact with through avenues other than language. Rocks and tables are also easily distinguished from their surroundings by the senses. But even with things like rocks and tables, there are different ways we might talk about those things (like "those things" or "minerals" or "landscaping materials" or "computer desk" or "platform").

Even with the simplest uses of a word, there are implications for speakers and audiences. If, for example, people refer to their partners by their role rather than their name ("the wife" is calling me), they foreground qualities, duties, and responsibilities of that role over other aspects of their relationship. If people refer to their partners using terms of endearment ("honey-pumpkin, can you get the phone?") they foreground their affections for that person. Labels for persons are not the only way implications about intimacy may be made; the way we label body parts and sexual desire ("Mr. Happy would like to see you") or sexual activities ("fool around," or "making love," or "do"—as in "do me," or "hit"—as in "I hit that") also matter in and have implications for our larger understanding of what's going on.[9]

Like labels, the metaphors we use to describe the sexes and sexuality also have their impact. Some metaphors (e.g., "women are the earth") can be both helpful and hurtful. They can be both rich in positive implications (women are foundational, women are generative), but also limiting in the way people are led to think and act (women are to be used for planting male "seed," women are passive "ground," women are not transcendent). Other metaphors may not be so overtly stated, but are revealed in language and action. For example, if a person speaks of sex in terms of exchange ("If I want that car, I'm going to have to put out") it reveals the metaphor "sex is a bargaining chip." If a person talks about a relationship or marriage as if it were a job, complete with duty, hierarchy, and a punch clock ("I've got to go put in some time with 'X,'"; "the 'boss' wants to see me"), then laborious aspects of the relationship and relations within it are highlighted. These metaphors aren't just verbal turns of phrase, like something used in an English class to make essays more artful or interesting: they are deeply influential. They can be so embedded in our minds that we don't even realize they're having an effect on how we think, what we think we know, and the way we act.[10]

Narratives, too, shape the way we make sense of sex and intimacy. This is because people like to fit in—to be like others and do things like others. Popular narratives (stories, myths, sequences of events), like those repeatedly recited in films and videos, on television, and in other temporal (time-organized) media, generate expectations. These expectations are often "habitual" or "unconscious" expectations about behavior, and Disney is as guilty as the pornography industry is in crafting narratives against which people compare themselves. "Are we on a 'date,' and what does that mean in terms of behavior?" "Are we doing what other people do when they have sex?" "Will we 'live happily ever after' now that we've finally found each other?" "Are you my 'one true love?'" Questions and concerns such as these can affect the way people make sense of what they do, and can throw added worries into intimacy besides the more immediate interests, concerns, and satisfactions of the people involved.

For instance, in the United States during the "sexual revolution," the combination of new and alternative sexual narratives and the desire to fit in led to significant personal and social turbulence. The explosion of public stories about sexual practices celebrating "free love" and "liberation," and the broader range of sexual experimentation featured in sexual stories, led some people who had otherwise been satisfied with their sex lives to question their sexual practices, and sometimes also their sexual relationships. People looking back at these times often express ambivalence about the effects these discourses had on their everyday intimate lives and sexual practices.[11]

Trying to change the way we *think* about a thing or event may require changing the way we t*alk* about a thing or event. But, changing the way we talk about a thing or event does not guarantee a change in attitudes or beliefs or actions. If a person decides to call sex "making love," even though they're having sex for sport, the renaming is at best a failure, and at worst a lie. If a person thinks a relationship is a roller coaster because of past experiences and/or the way relationships are usually portrayed in daytime TV soap operas and romance novels, then it would be hard to change this way of thinking simply by talking differently. Understandably, people who say things like "It's been a wild ride" and "I'm hanging on through the ups and downs" may have a harder time thinking of relationships as anything other than roller coasters. But becoming aware of how we talk about sex, sexuality, and sexual relationships is a first step toward recognizing how we think about things. And once we recognize how we think about things, we may have a better chance, if warranted, of being able to think and act otherwise.

It is a challenge to rewrite or create entirely new narratives to live by, other than those regularly offered by the culture (including those offered by one's own family). We know that myths of the perfect storybook wedding, the ideal engagement scenario, and the perfect life trajectory are so powerful that they can be difficult to resist, even when life is telling us very different stories. The same is true for narratives of sexual intimacy. Ideal sex, as portrayed in sex manuals and R-rated movies, often does not fit with real-life couples (especially when so few stories depict contraceptive use), and sex scenes in pornographic films can erroneously celebrate or stigmatize certain acts or activities, and mislead people about what might be desirable practices for particular real people. Often, the narratives our culture offers us are less than inspiring, or take us in the wrong directions. It may be wise, then, to re-craft popular narratives so that they better reflect ethical sexual relations, and our own understandings of sexual intimacy. Such re-crafting can be a healthy response to an unrealistic, overly conventional, and/or twisted culture.

In the following pages, I offer a few alternative metaphors of sex and sexuality, and a response to a dominant narrative that has implications for sex and sexuality. I do this to illustrate how people might go about counteracting and/or rethinking some of the more common (and less useful or responsible) sexual discourses of our time. I do not claim that my alternative metaphors and narrative critique are the "only" or "best" ways to think about and deal with sex and sexuality, but I do think they're better than much of what we hear all the time. They also try to show, in their implications and detail, how fruitful this sort of critical and creative thinking can be.

## The Gatekeeper

Despite the dangers to both men and women that are related to taking on multiple sex partners, heterosexual men are still scolded less for promiscuity than are women. When men sleep around, they are sometimes celebrated or envied as lady-killers or studs, while women who sleep around are more often pitied, criticized, or denigrated. We call this the double standard between men and women, and while it has eroded somewhat, it persists and continues to be a sticking point between the sexes. How can men and women relate well to each other sexually, when they are held to different standards of behavior? And how can we make sense of the differences between the sexes without coming to sexist conclusions?

One way to avoid sexist conclusions is to recognize that the different and stricter standard of behavior applied to women is not due to any "innate nature" of women. Historically, the innate nature of women has been defined in multiple and often unattractive ways. When paternity was first discovered, men who feared their own death became especially concerned about their own children, and patriarchy was born.[12] Concern over whose genetic material was being cared for placed women and children into the category of property, and required the policing of female sexuality through marriage, inheritance laws, and harsh laws against adultery. Christianity and other religions often vilified women and women's bodies, associating them with the profane and the ungodly, while the church became a stand-in for so much of what the feminine and maternal used to represent.[13]

Men who feared female power (or who envied or resented women's sex/sexuality) characterized women as hypersexual, primitive and uncivilized, or wily and dangerous tricksters who would use their sex as a means toward male ruin. Benevolent and patronizing men labeled women passive and childlike, unable to think rationally or for themselves (often a lie, but sometimes partly true—a consequence of the denial of education, self-sufficiency, and experience). In order to keep these "natures" in check, it was argued, women needed to be controlled, contained, steered, and dominated. This meant keeping women under the control of their fathers, husbands, or other male relatives; keeping women chaste before marriage; limiting a woman's education and experience; limiting women to a narrow set of acceptable sexual and social practices; and severely punishing women for any deviations from sexual and social norms and expectations.

These "innate natures" of women are inventions of culture and of history; they are not essential qualities. Some are contradictory (for instance, it is difficult to be both wily and irrational, or both passive and hypersexual). They have been used to rationalize the oppression of women for so long and to such an extent, that they have become naturalized. Because what people think of as "natural" to women (or to any human, for that matter) is heavily caught up in what culture tells us to think of as natural, we should always be aware of the lure of convenient—but potentially flawed—cultural stereotypes and consider that there are other, more appropriate explanations of why things are the way they are.

One less simplistic way of explaining the double standard considers not contrived "innate natures," but *consequences*. In other words, the double standard between men and women has more to do with what might happen as a *result* of sexual intimacy than it does with any innate nature that may be attributed to women by any particular social group or culture at any particular time in human history. Because women can get pregnant; because pregnancy, responding to a pregnancy, ending a pregnancy, and having a baby are physically, financially, and psychically demanding processes; and because women can get sexually transmitted diseases more easily from men than men can get them from women, *a woman has more at stake* when being sexually intimate with a man than a man has at stake when being sexually intimate with a woman. This is the reason why women "play defense" or often "should" play defense if they want to act in their own best interest when facing possible intimacies with a man.

Some might argue that there's little difference between "innate nature" and consequences. After all, it's a female's nature—her biological capacity to conceive—that leads to the (more serious) consequences she may face if she has sex. But the matter of nature is not so simple: biology is itself complex, biology has many ways of translating into social life, and biology translates in different ways, based on different situations.[14] In a capitalist society, fertility can be seen as a problem, because it interferes with productivity of female workers. But in a subculture where disease is treated, promiscuity is rare, conception is voluntarily managed, and resources are abundant, conception and pregnancy may be quite welcome (and its absence, rejection, or medical impossibility seen as a loss). To be sure, conception and pregnancy are significant to all humans and to any culture, but biology is complex, and it is not simply destiny. Personal qualities that people have do not bloom directly or only from one source, capacity, or experience. Women make babies, yes—but not all women make babies, and women are not continually, solely, or only baby makers and mothers.

The imbalance of possible consequences in heterosexual sex does not mean that women are passive and men are active. Neither does it mean that women need to be sheltered and protected by men so that other men can't "get at" them. What it means is that it is wise for women to initially be on the defense when it comes to sexual intimacy.

This way of understanding the sexual double standard suggests a few metaphors. One of these relates sex to football. When a football team wins the coin toss, they choose the most advantageous way to start the game. They assess the direction and force of the wind, sun, or other factors when deciding whether to kick off or start on defense. So, too, do women who have at least some control over what gets done sexually in a relationship need to "assess the winds, sun, or other factors," and take the most prudent course in terms of their own welfare. No knowledgeable football fan would suggest that defensive linemen are passive or unintelligent, or that they need special protection or sheltering because they play defense (all players need protection). What the metaphor does highlight is that there are many instances where choosing to play defense at the start of the game is the wisest course.

Another metaphor that may be appropriate to the double standard situation is the "gatekeeper" metaphor. In this metaphor, women are or need to be gatekeepers (at the "border" of their intimate "property"), while men, when they decide to, may "knock at the gate." As with the football metaphor, this way of seeing the sexual situation highlights women's activity. Women keep the gate closed, and/or decide when it is right to open it, and for whom. Men are also seen as active in this metaphor, and attention can be paid to the means they use to get through (or try to get through) the gate. Do they force their way in? Do they sneak their way in? Do they get themselves invited in? This metaphor doesn't deny the intimate property men also have and need to protect, but it does foreground the extra risks to which women are exposed when they engage in sexual intimacy.

The gatekeeper metaphor reflects not just the procreative potential of sex (assuming fertility, any man who "gets in" could make a baby), but also the social aspects of sex (sex is like a garden or a lawn to be enjoyed; a person who is let into a garden is special in some way). It acknowledges the inequality between the sexes regarding the consequences of sex, but does not overlook ways this inequality can be undermined or balanced out. For example, a man and woman who are committed to each other, using birth control, and sexually monogamous, or a man and woman who are married and in love and interested in conception, would be in a different "gatekeeping" situation than a couple considering sexual relations for the first time. In more secure and familiar contexts, reduction of possible negative consequences can lead to more sexual equality—and clear-cut "roles" of offense (gate-knocking) and defense (gatekeeping) may erode. It is in these contexts that we can better see heterosexual men's sexuality as its own desirable garden, with its own gate. Or perhaps an entirely new metaphor would be in order.

In the case of perpetual Don Juan-ism, on the other hand, the idea of the male as sole knocker-on-the-gate is reinforced. Such men may get tired of all the uptight women who won't "open up" (fixating on the gate instead of considering the owner of the garden), and the women they encounter may get tired of all the sex-fixated men. Under these circumstances, sexist stereotypes multiply: "women are frigid," and "all men care about is sex." A little more commitment would likely help this situation—not the sexist sort of commitment where lineage-minded men demand fidelity of (only) women (or of "their" women), but the mutual sort of commitment, where sexual equality within a relationship reduces or eliminates the adversarial nature of gatekeeping (and encourages garden parties).

## The Duck Pond Game

Consider how most people talk about sex in relation to courtship:

Is sex "hooking a fish"—the result of courtship, which is like fishing? Have you been throwing a lot of them back? Are there plenty of good fish in the sea? Or are they all bottom feeders? Are there too many sharks in the water? Do you try to lure a catch with shiny falsehoods? And if so, what is sex? Is it hooking a fish and wrestling it to the boat—or is sex the death of the fish? And what will you do now that you've preserved the fish carcass and hung it over the mantel? Is this a trophy husband or wife? Does it still provide a thrill, or do you want to go out and lure a new fish (or dip your paddle or fishing pole once again), in search of another thrill of the catch, or a bigger or better fish?

Is sex "the kill"—the result of courtship, which is like the stalking of big game? Were you tracking him or her down? Did you have him or her in your sights? Were you stealthy, lying in wait and then making your move? Did you pounce on a victim who never had a chance? Did you isolate the weakest one in the herd? And which part of the kill, exactly, is sex? Is it the mortal wound? Is it the death of the animal? Is it the rush you get when you "hit it" or "take it down?" Is one kill enough to satisfy, or, as with fishing, do you just want to go out and do it again—"bag" an even bigger and better trophy?

Is sex "the score"—the result of courtship, which is like a game? Did you outwit your opponent(s)? Did you get to the finish line first? Did you come away from the table a winner? Did you play your best hand? Did you play fair, or was there a trick or two up your sleeve? Did you get to first base? Did you get to second or third base? Did you score? Or did you take one for the team? And if sex is what you get for winning, then do you want to play again, or was getting the sex pretty much the goal? Will winning at the sex game be forever a competition with your partner, or with others? If the activity loses its competitive edge, will the game get boring and be too easy?

Is sex "the victory"—the result of courtship, which is like war? Did you use effective strategies and tactics? Did you overwhelm his or her defenses? Did you gain an advantage when his or her defenses were down? Did you take aim carefully? Are you the winning side who gets to take the spoils of war? Does this mean your partner is the loser? What happens when the war is over? Will sex always be seen as the result of a battle? Or is the vanquished side always now vanquished—and no longer interesting? That is, does victory leave you thirsty for more and different conquests?

All the familiar courtship metaphors just mentioned are weak when it comes to sex. Highlighting adversarial and competitive aspects of intimacy, they limit the imagination when it comes to intimacy, equating sex with death or loss or the ending of a process of action. Such ways of thinking and talking about sex are not simply harmless or irrelevant linguistic habits, nor are they simply poetic but superficial turns of phrase; they are reality-affecting metaphors and related statements that help shape the way we understand what sex is and what sex means to us as humans.

So here is an alternative sex metaphor to consider: sex is the duck-pond game. The duck-pond game is the game at carnivals where plastic yellow ducks circle around in a tub of water. Each duck has a number marked on its underside, and each player of the game gives their ticket and picks a duck. No matter what duck is picked, a prize is won. Whether the prize is simple and small, or elaborate and huge, the player is guaranteed to win something just by playing. Sexual intimacy could be seen this way, because the duck-pond game metaphor is not such a far cry from existing metaphors. Participants are, at the least, "in a game." The more they play, the more likely they are to win a big prize. Knowing they'll always win *something*, however, keeps the focus more on process than on product—more on the fun of the game in general—and not on winners or losers.

Like other game metaphors for sex, the duck-pond game highlights the social aspects of sex, but it leaves room for the procreative (a baby being a possible "prize" of sex). The duck-pond game metaphor also does not foreground violence, competition, or killing. Such a metaphor suggests the larger metaphor "courtship/relationship is a carnival," a fun place where people might go to enjoy rides and food and other games and events. The duck-pond game is thus part of the carnival experience, but one of a number of other experiences to be had (just as sex is only one part of intimacy). The essence of the duck-pond game is that every duck is a winner: every duck has a number on it, so as long as people play the game, they are guaranteed to win something.

Obviously, the metaphor just discussed does not accurately reflect all aspects of sex, nor does it represent all kinds of sexual encounters. The same, however, could be said of the more conventional sexual metaphors previously mentioned. What the alternative metaphor does offer is a different way of thinking about sex. Thinking about sex in a new or different way, even if it's not yet being experienced (or being experienced that way), helps make room for the possibility of sex some day or in some way "being" that way.

What if people thought of sex less as a violent or deadly sport or competition, and more as a game of the sort that does not involve competition or loss? What if people were to think of sex in other constructive ways (for instance, "sex is dancing," "sex is an art")? What if people thought of sex as something that was mainly about shared time and space, and mutual gain? What would it take to make it so that all people having sex would in some way gain and rarely suffer from that activity?

If people can't see sex as the duck-pond game or sex as dancing or sex as an art, we may want to ask why that is. Maybe they are fully under the influence of the conventional adversarial understandings of sex described earlier, the ones where sex is a kind of death or loss or end. Maybe they could become aware of the dominant metaphors by which they operate? Maybe they could even talk themselves out of these dominant metaphors and into some that are more constructive? What else besides the duck-pond game or dancing or art could people come up with as a healthy way to talk about and think about sex?

# Editing Sexual Practice

Sexual intimacy often requires successful interpersonal communication, but communicating during and about sexual intimacy can be tricky, especially when some sort of change in behavior is desired. A metaphor for talk about sex that offers some useful implications is "interpersonal talk with a partner about sexual intimacy is (or is like) editing a person's writing." The implications of this metaphor get at some of the particular challenges faced when people try to use language to alter the sexual practices of their partners.

If you have ever tried to edit another person's writing, you know how difficult it can be. People are sensitive about their writing, because writing is a reflection of the writer's style, and it is personal. Maybe it has been some time since you wrote an essay, paper, letter, or even a résumé. But it may not be hard to recall a time when a teacher, friend, or editor roughly or severely criticized your work. Writers whose work has been edited by others may have some idea about how important it is to make humane comments, but there is no guarantee that a person whose work has been edited by others will show the same care when it comes time to return the editorial favor.

A good editor does not try to change a writer's style completely; he or she tries to improve on a writer's existing talents, while taking care to maintain the writer's authorial "voice." Good editors are also strategic in the ways they go about correcting flaws. Some editors write comments on paper or computer screens to avoid the intensity of face-to-face feedback. The distance offered by these media helps preserve the self-esteem of the person whose writing practices are at issue, and reduce embarrassment by suggesting corrections without direct confrontation and possible additional haggling. If writers have issues with editor's comments, they can bring these issues up at a comfortable moment some time later, or write comments back to the editor.

Editing sexual practice is a similarly challenging task. Asking someone to change an intimate practice is in some ways a challenge to his or her sexual style, which can be disturbing to that person's sense of self. Delicacy and deftness in such matters is important, and being able to take criticism well is as important as being able to give it well. When successful, sexual "editing" has a similar outcome to those who learn from the editing of their writing—improvement and increased skill. With careful feedback, couples, with each other as audience, can enhance their sexual artistry, and maintain a rich and fulfilling sex life.

Like good editors of text, good "sexual editors" are honest. This means it is good to be honest about sex (to avoid lying—and that includes avoiding faking pleasure or orgasm). It is also important to be gentle with criticism. Some of a person's sexual style may be innate (sexual orientation in some cases, or hormone or pheromone-linked inclinations, for example), but even learned leanings are deeply ingrained, and no less deeply felt (say, cultural and religious taboos). Asking for changes in sexual practice that challenge a person's sexual style should be done with extreme caution and care. Celebrating a person's existing practices and talents and encouraging the creative expansion of those practices and talents may be less precarious ways to proceed.

Good sexual editors are strategic in the ways they go about addressing "flaws" or stylistic issues of intimacy. Respect for proper timing of comments is important, as is close attention to both verbal and nonverbal reactions of a partner. Sometimes euphemism or delicacy of wording helps minimize hurt feelings.[15]

In some cases, good sexual editors must make a judgment call about the quality of the intimacy, or the sexual compatibility of a partner. In instances where children are not part of the equation, the quality of sexual intimacy may loom large as a factor of and rationale for relationship. People whose sexual intimacies are mainly recreational may be especially inclined to keep or get rid of sexual partners based on those partners' sexual talents and compatibilities. People who have premarital sex also may use sexual compatibility as a reason for pursuing or avoiding a more involved relationship. Newly married couples who have not had premarital sex may have a more of an uncharted "editorial" situation than couples who have had sex before marriage, but love and attentiveness can do much to help the situation. In any event, the more people take seriously the quality of their sexual intimacies and their roles and responsibilities as honest, thoughtful, and ethically responsible sexual editors, the more satisfactory their sex lives are likely to be.

# Get a Grip

Men are active and women are passive. Men are the sky and women are the earth. Men are day and women are night. Men are rational and women are emotional, men are strong and women are weak, and so forth. The word "binary" is used when a group is split into two opposite parts that have no overlap, like the zeros and ones of computer code, or odd and even numbers. Human males and females are not binary, even though the way we are talked about makes it seem so.[16] Let us set aside this binary understanding of men and women for just a moment, and consider the following:

Women's and men's bodies are not opposite. Women and men both have livers and kidneys and bile ducts and shin bones, and we share a majority of chromosomes and many of the same hormones, though in somewhat different proportions. Neither are women's and men's private parts opposites, nor do they perform opposite functions. A vagina is not an "inside-out penis," as early theorists once claimed, and both sets of "plumbing" are part of reproductive and pleasure-generating human experiences.

Neither are women's and men's bodies opposite when it comes to sex acts. Both men and women enjoy touch, have erogenous zones (many of which are the same), have hands and tongues, etc. In all but the most depraved forms of sex, both men and women move around and do things. This means women are not necessarily "passive" during sex, any more than men are necessarily passive when women are in sex positions on top of men. The workings of a woman's internal sex-related muscles may not be as obvious or as telltale as a man's erection, but they can be just as much a part of sexual intimacy. Even the expression "lame fuck" suggests that at least some heterosexual men would opt for sex that includes a woman's active physical contributions (sex with a lively partner who is into it) over sex that does not include those contributions.

To help undermine the oppositional binaries between men and women perpetuated by this culture, and especially the active/passive binary, I offer an alternative metaphor for women and their privates: Instead of thinking of women and their privates as a hole, or a void, a space, a receptacle, or a passive vessel, people could think of women and women's privates as "grippers" that "grip" men during sexual intimacy.

Consider what this alternative metaphor offers. There are better grips and worse grips, and some of the success of grip has to do with the combination of the gripper and gripped. This draws attention to the issue of fit, which is a significant physical matter but seldom discussed in U.S. culture beyond gossip and dirty jokes. Despite claims made on late-night TV advertisements made by cute and sexy paid advocates for penis enlargement pills that "a man can never be too big," sometimes a man *can* be too big or too small. We should equally say a woman can be too big or too small.

The grip metaphor highlights that some success or failure in sex may be caused by size difference. This sexual variable is discussed in the *Kama Sutra of Vatsyayana*, where "hare men," "bull men," and "horse men" are put in sexual combination with "deer women," "mare women," and "elephant women" (a creative way of saying there are small, medium, and large sizes of each sex). Vatsyayana points out that the easiest match for intercourse is between people of the same size who "fit" together easily. One size removed also works, but different sexual positions are recommended to enhance comfort and sensation. More than one size removed presents challenges.[17]

Grip is not all or only the result of "fit"; it is also, more generally speaking, an active thing. The metaphor of "grip" points to sexual practices besides intercourse (that is, sex practices that would not lead to pregnancy) and also the way women can use their sex-related muscles to grip a partner. Hands have been popular sex organs for centuries, and oral sex has been more of an option for both men and women in this country ever since the women's movement, lesbian and gay rights movements, and increased talk about sex during the 1960s and 1970s led heterosexuals into broader territories of sexual practice and experimentation.[18] Grip is also relevant to intercourse. Since a woman is more than a vessel in this metaphor, success partly relies on the quality of her active participation. Women need to "get a grip," so to speak, and perhaps do what they can to improve their grip thorough Kegel exercises, positions, or movements.

This grip metaphor reminds women (as golfers and baseball players are often reminded), that a good grip can make all the difference in both technique (swing) and performance (results). Yes, it's important to have an adequate bat or golf club—one that is "fitting" to the occasion. But that is only part of the equation. The value of a baseball bat or a golf club is measured not just by its inherent properties, or by the success it might bring to *any* athlete, but by the grip of the particular athlete who actually swings it. (This helps explain how athletes can get attached to particular pieces of equipment, even those of older design and made of simple materials). Better golfers, baseball players, archers, lacrosse players, and cricket players, for example, do not treat their golf clubs, mitts, bows, sticks, or bats as mere tools. Smart athletes value, cherish, and even "become one" with their equipment.

Obviously, there is a problem of objectification here, of thinking of men or their private parts simply or merely as tools. But if we realize metaphors are useful precisely because they are not exact descriptions, then we can see the value of the "grip" metaphor, despite its limitations. We already see limitations and problems of objectification in existing sexual metaphors, such as the popular one where women are vessels passively receiving the (potentially pregnancy-generating) fluid contribution from an (active) male. And we don't have to abandon the vessel metaphor in order to accept the grip metaphor. But it might be a good idea to expand the kinds of metaphors available to describe sexuality and its meanings, especially because the meanings of sex are not only reproductive, they're social. The advantage of the grip metaphor is that it highlights the interpersonal aspects of sex, and the active nature of women as intimate sexual partners.

When it's time for intimacy, a man may plow and sow the field, dip his dipstick, stir the honey pot, wrap his package (and mail it), conquer territory, and sow his seeds. But both men and women should realize that women are not simply fields, oil pans, vessels, mailboxes, lands, or fields. These dominant and somewhat objectifying metaphors are difficult to challenge head-on, because they are so entrenched, and often quite useful. But what people can do, individually and in public discourses, is make use of new metaphors that recognize female agency. This is why the grip metaphor is useful. It encourages women to get a grip, become one with their equipment, and develop, in a happy and healthy way, their technique and follow-through. It offers a social, rather than solely procreative, focus, and a more active way for women to envision their role in a wide range of intimate sexual acts.

# For Singles: "I Don't Date"

Some people don't want to date. These people may be older singles with family, career, or other important matters to attend to, or they may be people of any age who just want or need to be on their own for a while. Sometimes moving to a new town can result in unwelcome attention as the "new single kid on the block." Or people may have had a recent relationship or marital breakup, or have recently lost a spouse or partner, and find themselves with newfound (and sometimes unwelcome) popularity. It's not always easy (it takes time) for people to shift from thinking of themselves as "taken" or "past their prime," to thinking of themselves as eligible and desirable, especially after years of being, thinking, or feeling otherwise. It is also not easy for people who have little or no previous experience with the dating scene to know how to deal with single people who now may find them interesting.

Attention, kindnesses, and popularity can be reassuring and welcome when a person is lonely or new in town, or after a difficult breakup or loss. But gestures of friendship and camaraderie sometimes come with intimacy "strings" attached, or may mask less virtuous motives and intentions. This can be true whether interested parties are way older or younger than is desirable, or if they come from such a different background and social milieu that it may really be a stretch to find common interests, or even if the ages are close and compatibility seems likely. When a person is single, it can be nice to be in the company of others. But this also means it can be a challenge dealing with others' romantic interests, and the disappointments that may result when issues of dating arise.

One tactic to use when faced with these situations is to let any and all interested people know: "I don't date." A person can start by just repeating the words aloud: "I don't date." In some cases, further clarification may be needed. For instance, it may be necessary to explain that "I don't date" does *not* mean "I'm willing to skip the 'playing games' part of relationship building and go straight to the 'having sex' part of things."

The "I-don't-date" tactic may result in some confusion at first. Likely responses include:

"What do you mean, you don't date?"

"Do you mean you won't date me, or do you mean you don't date anybody?"

"Why don't you date?"

"How can a nice, attractive, interesting person like you not date?"

"Aren't you unfairly robbing other people of the chance to get to know you?"

"But I really like you!"

There are many ways to respond to these questions and comments, but in any event, it is helpful if the answer is given cheerfully. People can simply reiterate the mantra, or they can explain that it's just a personal policy for the time being. They might say that they just need to take a break from dating for a while, or say they just don't really like the way dating is defined and understood, and spell out all the expectations that they think go along with the term (this level of explanation may be wise in only a few special instances).

The underlying rationale for the "I-don't-date" tactic has to do with the way dating is defined and understood. In many people's minds, dating is a complex and detailed narrative—a time-related, story-like ritual that generates numerous expectations that may be fulfilled or disappointed. Worries about dating proliferate: What is appropriate to wear? Where do we go and what do we do? Who picks up whom or do we meet there? Is the "date" walked to the car door? Are restaurant doors opened? Are chairs pulled out? Who pays for the date? Who calls whom afterward for another date? When (how soon after the date) is it appropriate to call (to make another date)? When is it appropriate to kiss? When (after how many dates) is it time to have sex?

The baggage of the dating narrative is not easy to work around, and the strict role-playing associated with it does little to foster real attentiveness toward other people and who they are. This is one reason why so many people meet new romantic partners at work or in other group contexts, where shared interests and activities are the focus. In these everyday contexts, sex is a much more remote matter, which means people can get to know each other's general qualities, interests, and talents with less distraction. Work and group contexts are also places where people can see how others react when they're angry or under stress, and how they treat friends and strangers. So by choosing social relations that are more like coworker relations, or by seeking out overtly non-dating group situations, there may be more of a chance for people to act and react more like themselves, and cut back on scripted expectations of intimacy.

Does this mean that a person who says "I don't date" writes off being sexually intimate? No, but this news needn't be advertised. Any person who fails to honor someone's wishes on this matter, makes unwelcome moves, or pushes alcohol as a means toward conquest should probably be avoided.

Does this mean that a person who says "I don't date" will never be someone's boyfriend, girlfriend, or partner? No, but this news needn't be advertised, either. A person can always decide to cancel the policy and go back to dating, or simply go straight into a relationship without dating. (In that case, new "rules of the road" can be established. and an original narrative of dating can be designed together by the couple).

The point of saying "I don't date" is to avoid the baggage of dating, not to avoid socializing and companionship entirely. This means that someone who says "I don't date" can still say, if he or she so chooses to do so, "... but I'll go get food with you," "... but we can go to the festival together," or "... but you can come to the party I'm having this weekend," and so on. If an activity is suggested, it should be easily afforded by the less affluent member of the duo. That way, each person can pay his or her own way for any expenses—or take turns treating for things so that there are no financial (and thereby implied social or interpersonal) inequities or obligations.

If real affinities between people exist, then so too should a willingness to hang out together (to share food, spend time, etc.), even if "dating" is not how the activity is defined. In such contexts, real friendship can develop, which is itself valuable. This friendship may (or may not) transform into a future relationship, sexual or otherwise, but there is no expectation that it will—or at least the person who says "I don't date" has been honest about how there should be no expectation that it will. In any event, sticking to the "I-don't-date" mantra helps a person stay single when they want to be single, as well as avoid those people who only want to follow the narrative and perform the roles of dating, with all the baggage and all the expectations that go with them.

# Making Good Sex More Likely

There are some things that make sex more likely (and more fun), and other things that make sex less likely (and less fun). Some of these things depend on the kind and the length of relationship people are in—Is it a one-night stand? Is it a more serious love relationship?—while other matters apply more generally, depending on the particular situation (is the person's onion breath distracting?). Having a good time sexually can also become part of people's memories, which can inspire a willingness to have more sex and be more experimental (often with the same person who helped make the good memories). Good sex can't repair broken relationships, nor can it act as the sole foundation of love relationships. But good sex can enliven, enrich, and reinforce interpersonal relationships, including love relationships, in concrete and tangible ways.

Some things that make sex more likely are positive feelings toward one's partner, fitness, good hygiene, having time to devote to being intimate, and having the right setting and supporting materials for intimacy.

Few things make it easier to want to be intimate than real positive feelings toward a partner. For some people, only love sanctions intercourse and related activities. For others, friendship or liking can be enough. In any case, it is important to address any hidden resentments or hostilities that may interfere with warm feelings toward a sex partner. It is also important to frequently take inventory of and be grateful for things that one member of a couple does for the other, or for the couple as a unit, or for family and community, and to keep those things in the foreground of the mind. It is easy to take other people for granted, and to become so attentive to one's own contributions and tasks, that what others do for us and for those around us is forgotten. Meditating a bit on what one really likes or loves about an intimate partner, and about past enjoyable experiences and other positive memories, can do a great deal to set a good mental and emotional mood for physical intimacies.

Keeping fit is also important to a healthy sex life. This does not mean that sex is necessarily better for skinny people and athletes. What it does mean is that a certain amount of stamina and flexibility are an advantage to sexual intimacy. Being able to try out new positions, or being able to "go at things" for a while (or more than once), is only possible if a person is fit enough and has the energy. Looking good (including staying at a reasonable weight) is also often appreciated. This does not sanction superficial or dangerous means of self-alteration (that is, Botox injections, extreme weight training, bingeing and purging, plastic surgery, liposuction, extreme dieting, steroid abuse, and so forth). But it does underscore the importance of a healthy diet and regular exercise. Enough people who start even mild exercise programs and better eating habits say they consequently experience not only a stronger sex drive but an improved sex life. These sex-related changes are not the only reasons why people might want to stay healthy, but they're good ones.

Good hygiene can mean different things to different people, in different cultures, and at different times in history. Some people shower every morning, some do not. Some people shave various parts of their bodies, some do not. Scents found desirable by some people may be offensive to others, and arguments seldom change these olfactory sensibilities. Hygienic practices some people might think of as "normal" or "natural" may be though of by others as "barbaric," "primitive," "weird," or "uncool." Fads complicate what is considered proper, and because so many hygienic practices are rooted in custom, there is no way to know the truth about what is appropriate. What couples can do is to carefully and gently communicate about matters of hygiene so as to maximize turn-on and minimize turn-off. This usually involves sharing or explaining rather than ultimatums, and can be negotiated either before intimacy ("I love the way 'X' perfume/cologne smells on you ..." or "In general, I like it or find it a turn-on when you shave your face or legs, because ..."), or during intimacy ("Since you're freshly showered, let's ...").

Having or making the time to be intimate is also important. This doesn't mean putting sex on a schedule, like a doctor's appointment or some other duty, but it does mean keeping sex in the forefront of possible fun things to do. It may also mean periodically finding out (by asking) what a partner thinks would be an ideal amount of sex/sexual intimacy per day, week, or month, what times of day are preferred, etc. Individuals may vary in their sense of an ideal, and not all ideals may be met, but compromises and understanding are more likely if each person in a couple has a sense of the other person's needs and desires.

Many people complain they don't have time for sex, but those same people often spend hours a day watching TV, checking Facebook, playing video games, or reading formulaic books and magazines. Such entertainments are often less demanding than sex, but they also may be less rewarding than sex. People who forego temptations such as these often discover not only that they have more time for sex than they thought, but also that their experience of time during sex seems to expand. This is because time is not just a measure or a unit, but a "felt" experience (as when time "flies" or "stands still").[19] For example, many enjoyable electronic pastimes (like watching a movie or playing video games) are fleeting. Even after hours have passed, it's easy to wonder where the time went. In contrast, enjoyable physical, sensual, participatory, and embodied experiences can feel "full," and as if they have gone on for a long time, regardless of actual duration. This is because the people involved are actively and holistically engaged in what's going on. And like the occasional win while gambling, the thrill of the fortuitous and perhaps unexpected sexual happening (say simultaneous orgasm, or the discovery of a new technique or position) can magnify the sense of time passed by means of physiological pleasures experienced.

Making time for intimacy is especially challenging for people with children. Kids make it difficult to have time (and space) for intimacy, and it is no secret that the demands of child rearing can put strains on even the most loving of couples, including strains on intimacy. Much has been written about the need for couples to leave the kids with Grandma and take a few days off to themselves. This is often easier said than done. Not everyone has a convenient grandma, and it is often difficult to "power down" and go back to practices of "couple-hood," once the practice of parenting is under way. Still, the advice to take time to be intimate should not be ignored, especially by people who have taken delight in such practices in the past, who have had it contribute positively to their relationship before, and who know how satisfying it can be.

Finally, it is important to have the right setting and supporting materials for intimacy. Effective birth control is not only an ethical necessity for those who do not wish to conceive, it is also key to relaxation (as in a lack of worry about pregnancy). Relaxation is an important part of many people's idea of a good setting. Condoms can reduce worries about sexually transmitted diseases (though condoms can break, and they can also dull sensations). Some people have suggested that women's sexuality is more responsive to environmental factors, while men's sexuality is more directly tactile. More specifically, the claim is that physiological relaxation is needed for women to achieve sexual arousal and climax, whereas for men, arousal and climax are more directly related to certain kinds of stimulation of certain parts of the body. But it has also been observed that, when masturbating, most men and women can bring themselves to climax in around the same amount of time (four minutes or so, on average).[20] It is also known that stress negatively influences both men and women's sexual state of mind. So, whether differences in needs for stimulation or relaxation are rooted in the body (for instance, in the physiology of orgasm), or in the mind and situation (in assumptions about masculinity and femininity, worries about pregnancy, concerns about pressing career- or household-related matters, etc.), they may be worth noting and addressing.

Other matters of setting will depend on the people involved. Some people feel more at ease having sex or trying new sexual activities in their own homes, bedrooms, or beds. Others may prefer experimenting in an out-of-town location—or in beds that someone else will have to make or change. While travel can be liberating, it is also important to take along any needed supplies. Some people may like mood-setting rituals or practices (special lighting, pre-intimacy bath or shower, etc.). Because women often do laundry, they may have concerns about bedding and stains, especially at certain times of the month. Some people may want to be near a bathroom if they feel the need to wash up or shower before or after intimacy. Some people may need condoms, spermicides, or contraceptive appliances. Some may want easy access to sex toys. Some people may need ready access to lubricants, especially if medications, menopause, or other factors would make intercourse painful without it. A wastebasket might be desired, or handy tissues or towels. All of these factors, and more, are part of the sexual scene, and may help or hinder any particular encounter. It is up to the people involved to be clear about what enhances and what degrades the sexual setting, so that they can design inviting sexual contexts and more fully enjoy their intimacy, both at home and elsewhere.

## Endnotes

1. Arthur Asa Berger, 1998.
2. Josiah Royce, 1967.
3. See, for example, John Gray's (1995) discussion of his post-monk, premarriage sexual investigations, in which he asked various female sexual partners quite frankly and openly about their sexual likes and dislikes—and his discovery that this had a positive effect on their libidos.
4. For an example of failure in advice on this matter, see John Gray (1995). His list of 10 sexual turn-offs for men includes "ouch, that hurts" (p. 55). Gray recommends women avoid saying this, for fear it will undermine a man's sexual enthusiasm. But responding to sex-related pain is more important than maintaining sexual momentum.
5. William Masters and Virginia E. Johnson, 1966.
6. Arthur Asa Berger, 1998.
7. Robert Baker, 1975.
8. George Lakoff and Mark Johnson, 1980.
9. Robert Baker, 1975.
10. George Lakoff and Mark Johnson, 1980.
11. See Lillian Rubin's interview study and discussion of the "sexual revolution" in the United States in the late 20th century in *Erotic Wars*, 1990.
12. Leonard Shlain, 2003.
13. David Noble, 1992.

14. For example, some women are infertile, some have been sterilized, some take vows of chastity for religious reasons, some use birth control, etc.
15. See in this book "Appendix A: Euphemism and Alternative Wording Suggestions."
16. Valerie V. Peterson, 1997.
17. Vatsyayana, 1964.
18. John D'Emilio and Estelle B. Freedman, 1988.
19. John Poulakos and Takis Poulakos, 1999.
20. William Masters and Virginia E. Johnson, 1966.

# Part III

## Society

# Children

S ex is a social act, not only because it involves two people, but also because other people and potential people may be involved. Consequently, it is important for those who have sex to be clear about feelings and beliefs regarding the matter of pregnancy and children. If it is our responsibility, in social situations, to try to do less—instead of greater—harm to others, and less—instead of greater—harm to ourselves, then unintended pregnancies may present apparent conflicts of interest. "Harm to the other (e.g., abortion) might help the self/selves (for example, allow life plans to continue) or it may harm the self/selves (lead to complications, loss, regret, etc.). No harm to the other (e.g., having a baby) might be a harm to the self/selves (take a physical toll, take precedence over other life plans, etc.) or it may be a help to the self/selves (for example, give life purpose, open new horizons of experience). Weighing advantages and disadvantages against each other is difficult, because two people may have different ideas about what to do about an unintended pregnancy and different levels of power over the matter. Decisions are also made difficult when short- and long-term consequences of having a baby are hard to determine, laws and customs are in flux, and when the status of the entity to which harm might be done is infinitely debatable (would harm be done to a person? a baby? a fetus? And what sorts of rights should such an entity have?).

Responses to unintended pregnancy may be affected by age, marital status, financial status, emotional and mental fitness, desire for children, and how people comparatively value "innocent" (fetal) life in relation to experienced (adult) life. Other factors may include the relational circumstances in which pregnancy occurs (incest, rape, casual sex, monogamy, marriage) and the support systems that might be available, once a child is born. Also relevant may be the number of children already requiring care, work demands and career interests, cultural sex biases (usually against female offspring), and health issues (including potential or actual genetic or physical anomalies of the fetus discovered through amniocentesis or ultrasound; selective reduction during fertility treatments; and health threats to the life of the mother). In some cases (extreme poverty, lack of medical care, abusive circumstances), pregnancy is the only option.

When a child is planned for, or when a decision is made to bring a pregnancy to term, parents should do what they can to ensure the well-being of the developing child. This is especially true when what looks like something good for the parent is outweighed by something that would be good for the child. Leaving a pleasant, but low-paying, job to focus on a child's development (and save on child care) by becoming a stay-at-home parent is one example. Another is taking the time and trouble for prenatal care and counseling in matters of nutrition, exercise, education about the significance of toxins, practice for childbirth, and preparation for early parenting. Partners, cohabiting friends, and family may help with housekeeping (especially by taking the brunt of cleaning solvent effects), and by joining in on the reduction of or abstaining from nicotine, alcohol, and other dangerous substances, so as to further improve the fetal environment, or express solidarity with the expecting mother.

In recent years, the distancing of sex from marriage and a reduction in the social and economic value of children has taken its toll on parenting as a practice. While children born to parents who want them are a joy, an opportunity to grow, an entry point into important social circles, a chance to revisit youth, and perhaps even a bid toward immortality, those children born to a reluctant parent or parents may not be experienced or treated in this way. In modern urban and suburban contexts, children are more of an economic burden than an asset, unlike their counterparts of earlier times in agrarian settings. The cost of basics such as food, clothing, shelter, and education continue to grow; as everyday life becomes more and more complex, caring and providing for children presents added challenges. A parent's desire for personal growth can clash with the needs of children, and the mobility of the culture and fickle job market mean not only that it is hard for parents to stay afloat and support their children, but also that even the most healthy, talented, and responsible children may not be able to support their parent(s) in their old age. In a world full of meaningless suffering, terrorism, weapons of mass destruction, totalitarianism, and growing extremisms, even bids to immortality may lose some of their appeal.

For these and other reasons, modern industrialized nations have seen their birth rates slow to a crawl. If it weren't for its large immigrant population (and their higher birth rates), statistics would put the United States near the top of the list of least prolific nations. Deciding to have a small family or be a "no-kidder" is becoming more common, though the latter is still experienced as swimming against the stream of procreative or child-rearing expectations. Couples who are DINKs (Dual Income, No Kids) are also becoming more common. While people with children may pity no-kidders for the parenting experiences they lack, they may also resent the lifestyles that being a no-kidder makes possible. No-kidders are often highly engaged in their careers and professions. And many no-kidders are able to devote time and energy to social needs and causes beyond those presented by immediate blood ties.

In the face of all this, and despite challenges, child rearing is still one of the most fulfilling and fundamentally important of human practices. Unlike other animals that operate largely on instinct, humans must learn most of what they need to know after they are born. This means that parents play a significant role in the lives of their children, and that good parenting is integral to the welfare of individuals, communities, and culture. Parents need to do right by their children, attend to them, and give them time and energy. They also need to give the care of children precedence over other matters in their lives. But neither is it a good thing when a parent's life (including sexual life) is almost entirely sacrificed for the sake of child rearing or subsumed in a child's accomplishments. While love for a partner or talents and achievements can never substitute for the love parents feel for their children (or children for their parents), neither can the love of and for children substitute completely for these other passions.

# Innocence vs. Experience

I magine this hypothetical situation: You are the only adult in your home one night, and you wake up to a raging fire. Your two children, a newborn and a three-year-old, are in the house as well. Their bedrooms (two different bedrooms) are both extremely difficult to reach at this point, and their rooms are in different parts of the house. Help is nowhere in sight, and time is short. You will only be able to make it to one of the children's rooms before being overcome by heat and smoke yourself, and neither child can make it out of the house on his or her own. Which child do you try to save?

The answer people give to this question and the reasons they give to justify it say a good deal about priorities. Here are some rationales:

Go for the newborn, because the newborn hasn't had a chance to have any life yet, while the three-year-old has at least had three years of life to enjoy. Go for the newborn, because the newborn is more innocent—he or she has had less time on this earth to sin, and so is less "tainted," and thus more worthy of being saved. Go for the newborn, because he or she hasn't had a chance to develop a personality yet. Go for the newborn, because the qualities (characteristics, capacity level, personality) of the three-year-old are less desirable or undesirable, so it's better to take chances with what may exist or develop in the younger child, rather than sticking with the known qualities of the older child.

Go for the three-year-old, because he or she has had three years of life to enjoy, experience, learn language, and become self aware. Go for the three-year-old, because those three years have made that child into more of a defined and unique person, and this person is now more valuable because of that development. Go for the older child, because time, energy, and love have already been invested in childrearing, and losing the effects of that effort would be unfortunate. Go for the three-year-old, because the qualities (characteristics, capacity level) of the newborn are less desirable.

Underlying these different rationales are the different values people give to *innocence* and *experience*. If people value *innocence more than experience*, they would be more likely to oppose abortion rights and support wars that kill large numbers of foreign civilians. This is because they see inexperienced, but racially similar, people as *more valuable*, and "differently experienced" people as *less valuable* than average. If people value *experience more than innocence,* they would be more likely to support abortion rights and oppose wars that kill large numbers of foreign civilians. This is because they see experienced, but racially different, people as *more valuable*, and inexperienced and similar, but not-yet-developed, persons as *less valuable* than average. If people value innocence and experience about equally, then they could either be against both abortion and war in all cases, or be open to debate about the rightness or wrongness of a particular abortion or a particular war, depending on the situation.

Notice that both ways of prioritizing value discriminate. Those who lean toward *pro-innocence* discriminate against people who are "dirtied" by experience, while those who lean *to pro-experience* discriminate against people who are young or unaccomplished. This is why pro-innocence religious fundamentalists can support the death penalty, and at the same time condone terrorism and the torture of "evil others," and why the pro-experience ancient Greeks could practice infanticide with their own children, while taking vanquished foes from the battlefield into their homes as skilled slave labor.

If people value *experience more than innocence,* they might be more likely to oppose the death penalty, because they believe redemption is possible—that people or groups of people are never simply "good," "evil," or "evildoers." Or they may think that their own flaws make it inappropriate for them to participate in life-taking. This last rationale, by the way, also gives those who value experience a reason to reject abortion as a way to deal with unintended pregnancy, especially to the extent that they recognize a fetus as a life (which explains the attention paid to fetal development in current laws and litigation). But it does not rule out abortion as an option completely, especially when other factors of experience are part of the situation (pregnancy threatens the mother's life or the mother's future, pregnancy overwhelms resources of a family, pregnancy endangers the primary caregiver or breadwinner of the family, pregnancy arises early in a girl's life, pregnancy is the result of rape or incest, and so on).

We can see how these rationales play out in two cases: one publicly discussed, the other kept private. The public case concerns Sarah Palin and her daughter. Sarah Palin, John McCain's vice presidential running mate in the 2008 presidential election, has a daughter who had an unintended pregnancy shortly before and during her mother's bid for election. As a conservative Republican and conservative Christian, Palin's supportive response to her daughter's pregnancy exemplified the valuing of innocent life over experience.

The situation of Sarah Palin and her daughter, however, was somewhat different from situations many other Americans face. The father of the baby comes from an oil-rich family, and the Palin family is also well off and well connected. This means that financial support—and perhaps also social stigmatization—are not as much of a problem for the new mother as they might be for other women. When the election was lost and a marriage did not come to pass, the Palins were still not faced with much hardship. The father could provide child support, and both parents and their families could afford nannies, child care, and other services to help the new mother.

During her time as governor of Alaska, Sarah Palin helped erode abortion rights in that state for women, especially for poor women. The *innocence* of fetuses, and Palin's preference for that life, overrode the experience that young or grown women might have, and their right to judge for themselves and their families what to do with their lives.

A different story shows a situation where experience was valued over innocence. In this case, a woman was in college at the end of a four-year relationship. She had "rebound" sex with a casual acquaintance, the condom broke, and she became pregnant. With the support of her parents, she got an abortion, which she says she does not regret. She finished her degree, and started a career in a high-paying profession. Eventually, she met a man—a nice, loving, conservative, Republican man with a secure, high-paying job. They are now happily married, and have a loving home and two charming daughters. Because of his political party, this woman's husband is likely to vote against abortion rights. He doesn't know that an abortion is part of what shaped his wife's experience and helped make his current life possible. It's possible he'll never know about the abortion, and it's likely she'll never tell her story to a wide audience. It is also likely that this woman's situation is not unique.

People often like to privilege *innocence over experience* because it's easier—it offers more yes-or-no, black-or-white answers (e.g., "save all the innocent babies"). But conscious and unconscious hypocrisy is sometimes part of the (often untold) story. Valuing *experience over innocence*, on the other hand, is a messier and more complicated business. It demands attention to detail, honesty, thoughtful consideration and weighing of competing values and moral frameworks, and avoidance of easy, or simply self-serving conclusions.

We all value experience and we all value innocence, but when these values come into conflict, we find out to which one we grant the greater weight. How have your experiences shaped the way in which you lean? And how much do you know about what others have done and experienced?

# Family

The understanding of family varies across individuals and cultures. Some people see family as blood relations only. Others see family as an essential social unit, one that offers roles for participants, and emotional and financial support to its immediate or extended members. Still others see family as a loose set of people with whom they affiliate and share holidays.

For some, family means a "nuclear family," consisting of a mother and a father and their immediate offspring (who are the result of the blending of their own genetic material). For those who think of family in this way, other kinds of families are "unusual." Children from other relationships or marriages or sources (as in adoption) are seen as in some way peripheral, and unmarried persons are seen primarily as "children of their parents" (and part of the parents' family), no matter how old they get, and no matter what other sort of family they may claim.

For others, family is more broadly construed. It may be extended, and include blood relations beyond the immediate (such as cousins and grandparents), or it may include people who are not related by blood, but who have other good reasons for being together in a family: adopted children, friends, gay partners, people taken in, etc. How obligated a person feels to family and people in their family is partly the result of how they have been raised to feel about their family *by* their family, and also partly the result of other factors in their environment. Does a person feel any responsibility toward carrying on their genetic line or family name? Does a person feel any responsibility toward caring for elderly relatives? Does a person feel any responsibility toward following in their mother's or father's footsteps—or fulfilling their mother's or their father's desires or unfulfilled aspirations? Does a person feel any responsibility toward having parental blessings regarding friends or lovers? Many of the answers to these questions are so deeply ingrained and felt as to seem beyond dispute.

Two significant factors affecting the modern family in the United States are contraception and women in the workforce.[1] Contraception extends women's capacity to work by allowing for the control of fertility, and women who work are more able to take care of themselves financially. Developments in these areas have challenged traditional gender roles (especially the traditional breadwinner role of father), and they undermine the patriarchal nuclear family, especially within the lower and middle classes, where working women commonly (or must) work in order to provide for their children. In the face of these developments, the state often picks up the slack, providing services that the nuclear family's father used to provide (for instance, welfare, children's health care, schooling, and meal programs).

The erosion of the patriarchal nuclear family is further confirmed by the increasing numbers of blended families and by the growing numbers of women who choose not to marry upon discovering they are pregnant (although they may maintain ties or live with the father of their children, or take part in other family arrangements). While some people worry that weak nuclear families will leave men without an important place or role in society and make it easier for the state to raise patriotic "cannon fodder," others welcome the change as a natural outgrowth of the independence of females, which could result in more communal, intergenerational, and less insular ways of raising children.[2]

Do people have a responsibility to keep their family going? This is a difficult question, but despite the value of having a wide range of genes in the gene pool, people should not be obligated to carry on their genetic lines (even if their parents desire grandchildren). Because there is no shortage of humans today, a no-kidder stance may not only be forgivable, it may be ethical.[3]

If fuller variety in the gene pool is desired, other ways of accomplishing this goal may be pursued (say, increasing incentives for parenting for the desired group, reduced "penalties" for parenting for the desired group, encouraging sperm and egg donation from the desired group, and so on). On the other hand, none but the most profoundly unfit should be discouraged from reasonably participating in the gene pool. The eugenics movement in this country showed how encouraging notions of "good" genes and racial fitness played into the hands of white supremacists, and justified forced sterilization of racial minorities (not to mention other extremes of injustice). History shows that no one human virtue would be a virtue if it were the only one to be had, and sexual reproduction itself exists because sharing genetic material increases the fitness of a species by increasing that species' chances of creating a diversity of individuals.

In some parts of the world, infanticide is used to decide which children live, and which ones die. In many countries, the children eliminated are female, and the resulting male-heavy demographic can become a problem.[4] In other places, including the United States, reproductive technologies, such as genetic testing, amniocentesis, and ultrasound, give prospective parents a chance to monitor fetal development and make similar choices about life and death, using selective reduction and abortion. In many of these cases, choices are made against genetic and physical defects. In some situations, these decisions are made by individuals or couples, and supported by the state. In other cases, individuals come into conflict, and the state helps decide who wins; or couples come into conflict with the state, and the state decides what a person or couple can (and can't) do. Other forms of genetic and social control impacting the family are less direct, but they also have their influence. Tax credits and other governmental incentives for families with children, religious teachings and taboos, marriage laws, and health insurance coverage are all part of the situation.

In every human community, families are subject to explicit and implicit controls derived from a variety of sources. In every human community, people obey, make use of, resist, and ignore these controls. What is most important in a community is that people do their best to discover and develop their own special talents to enhance the well-being of the people around them. Whether or not this includes regularly keeping in touch with family, supporting (or helping support) a family, having and rearing children, adopting children, caring for children and adults, or providing some other good to the narrower or wider community is partly a matter for a person to decide, and partly beyond a person's control. It is the part within a person's control that should be considered carefully, in light of the part that is not.

# Two Out of Three

In the 1970s, many well-meaning feminists in this country tried to sell women on an optimistic dream. They said "You can have a man, you can have a career, and you can have children. You can—and should—have it all!" What these feminists failed to take into adequate consideration was biology, and the stubborn political system and culture of the United States.

Currently, the United States spends huge amounts of money, time, and energy on war, defense, and "empire maintenance," and much less money, time, and energy, proportionally, on health care, early education, and child care. The health care of children is left primarily to parents, and the answer to "Who gets care?" is still largely related to "Who is legally related to whom?" and "Who can afford to pay?" Primary and secondary school funding is linked to property taxes, and these taxes (and the investment in education they afford) vary widely from place to place. In some areas, public schools are so underfunded, overcrowded, and poorly administered and staffed, that they can provide neither safety nor minimal intellectual challenge. Parents who can afford to do so may send their children to private schools, but these schools face their own financial and administrative challenges. Parents may home school if they have the time and education to manage it, but many parents are not so fortunately endowed. Day care and other child-care services are mostly privatized, so only people who can pay for it (and pay for the best) can have it. Exceptions to these examples exist, but many are in the lowest socioeconomic brackets of society (for instance, child-protective custody is a form of health care or child care) and are not desirable options.

In other countries (some small European countries, for example), the state performs a rather different role. Partly because these countries don't (or can't) consider themselves the world's police officers, they spend a larger proportion of their tax revenues on the welfare of their own people. People in these countries often pay a higher proportion of their incomes in taxes, but this high proportion is perhaps easier to tolerate when the bulk of the money goes back into social services from which citizens directly benefit. The state acts more like a father (and mother) to children in these countries, providing health care (through various forms of universal or socialized health care), government-sponsored child care, and a somewhat more consistent and effective educational system for children.

Despite recent changes (such as health care reform), the United States is still far from the sort of situation just mentioned. The United States is a country of religious and ethnic diversity, so ideas about what makes a good educational system, and what and how students should be taught, vary across the population. Because this country holds equality in high esteem, excellence in academics is often undermined (we see how "no child left behind" easily slides into "few children excel" and "all students are above average"). The United States is so huge, that its sheer size makes it hard to design and run efficient and helpful social programs.

Many people in the United States also are not interested in giving the government any more of their money in taxes. They believe, often justifiably, that the government has spent their money badly in the past. Even if higher taxes and universalized health care improve the level of health care for many people in this country (and that's a big "if"), and even if universal health care would mean a more flexible relationship between individuals and their employers and career choices, it is unclear how "freedom-loving" U.S. citizens will adapt to a more community-style approach to health decisions. People might want universal health care, for example, but might also find it hard to agree about what counts as more or less "worthy" expenses (e.g., prenatal care vs. organ-farming research).

Combine the "you can have it all" idea with the political and cultural scene of the United States today, and you get a physically, mentally, and emotionally draining situation where women are trying to do too many things at once, and failing to do any of those things particularly well (or failing to do some of those things well, at the expense of other things). Without reforms, "having it all," for women, means mostly "having too much on one's plate." The hope that this generation of "superwomen" will gain enough political traction to change the culture, and the laws of the land, has largely faded. With so many significant responsibilities, and without additional help from extended family, it's hard for many women just to keep up with their own narrow territories of influence.

Men, meanwhile, have not had it much (if any) easier. The assumption that men had it all to begin with was false. Men who had a wife and children and who fulfilled the breadwinner role were often absent from the child-rearing project, and increased expectations about fatherhood do not come along with additional hours in the day to meet those expectations. Men who fulfill primary caregiver roles are still not fully accepted by the culture as primary caregivers, and men who share equally in child-care tasks with their partners are still subject to criticism from coworkers for being "distracted." Although some changes have been made in sharing responsibilities for housekeeping and child care, inequalities persist, even when incomes are commensurate. On the other hand, achieving equality by adding men to the list of people expected to "do it all" is not necessarily an improvement.

It takes time and energy to develop and maintain a love relationship between two people. It takes time and energy to be a good parent, and it takes time and energy to cultivate a career. And so, it may make sense to let women (and men) off the hook. What we might say is "you might *not* be able to have it all." We might say that "two out of three ain't bad." You can be in a love relationship and care for kids but have no career (or only a job); you can have kids and be divorced (or have a rocky relationship with your partner), and focus on being a parent and working at your career; or you can have a relationship and a career and be a no-kidder.

Two new challenges arise from this perspective. The first asks people to take stock of themselves, their talents, and their desires, and put their commitments into a hierarchy (one that may be adjusted, rarely, if need be, but one that is serious and life shaping). The second asks people to stay open to, make friends with, and learn from, not only those people who share in their territories of focus, but also—and especially—those who do not. The coalitions built with those latter "different" people are far more likely to bring about positive social and political change than all the special interest groups that so often simply work at cross purposes to each other, and cancel each other out.

Relationship, children, and career are not "things" over which people have complete control, but they do require attention, and they can be cultivated. If people are lucky, they might even end up "having" all three and "handling" all three well. If they do, they should consider themselves both resourceful and extremely lucky. In the United States, "having it all" should be the fantastic and celebrated exception—not the rule—or even the ideal, at least until the political and cultural environments are substantially changed.

By advocating that people scale back a bit, the "two out of three ain't bad" mantra by no means lowers the bar of human performance. If anything, it argues *against* mediocrity and *for* excellence, within a narrower set of territories. It calls for better parents and better partners and better professionals, and it tries to make the expectations that people put on themselves and their children more humane. It reminds people that they can live their lives well and fully, stay sane, contribute to society, and not have to feel guilty for not being all things to all people. Finally, it recognizes that if people pool their accomplishments as members of larger social units—that is, if they see themselves as friends and couples and members of communities—then together they *can and do* have it all.

# Eighty Cents' Worth

W hy is it that women in this country make only 80 cents for every dollar a man makes? Why has this proportion not changed much in the last few years? And why is it that women, as a group, are not promoted as often as men, even when their résumés show similar qualifications? Can women, as a class, ever achieve equal pay for equal work?[5] Considering the current political system in our country, and the importance of having well-cared-for children, the answer, perhaps not surprisingly, is no.

Discrimination is a complex practice inspired by a variety of motives, not all of them bad (people discriminate against milk that is past its expiration date and against convicted serial child molesters who apply to work at day-care centers). The question to ask about discrimination is not whether or not it exists, but whether or not it is fair or just. For women, discrimination is related to sex in a variety of ways, including sexual attractiveness, sexual harassment, and—most relevant here—the potential for pregnancy.

Even though not all women reproduce, women are that class of humans who can get pregnant, carry a child, and nurse a child. This is not a stereotype; it is a significant physiological difference. It leads to (but does not mandate) certain other social roles, specifically "primary caregiver."

Because the U.S. government does not contribute substantially to child care, and because citizens (of varied ethnic and religious backgrounds) might not trust the state to provide good child care even if it did, people in the United States, as citizens, have a choice: rely upon on mothers, parents, or other private institutions to raise children, or increasingly leave child rearing to the state. If people lean on mothers or parents to raise children, then they can demand equal pay for equal work for women's workplace labor only if they are also willing to accept, in theory and in practice, the logical extensions of these demands: equal breadwinning and equal child-care responsibilities for men and women.

Some men say they would like it if their wife or partner were the bread-winner of the family, but this does not always play out so well in actuality, and in the context of social groups. Other men tell their partners they will share equally in housekeeping and child-care duties, but once commit-ments are made, the women end up doing the bulk of the work, even when workplace demands and paychecks are equal. Some theorists suggest the male breadwinner role helps balance out women's larger physiological contribution to childrearing, and without it men would feel left out and less needed.[6] These observations do not mean equality is undesirable or impossible. They do mean, however, that it is important to be honest about what real change and real equality require.

If people want equal pay for equal work for women, they also should be willing to accept the likely consequences of this equality: a situation in which parenting will look comparatively less attractive than work outside the home for those with good jobs and good pay; a decrease in men's sala-ries in proportion to the increase in women's salaries (why pay a man to support an entire family when you can expect both parents—together—to make enough money to do so?); an increase in the number of families where one single parent, or both married or divorced parents work; and a possible a decrease in the amount of focus, time, and energy spent on parenting.

On the other hand, we can ask women to financially "take one for the team," meaning a woman would accept 80 cents of pay to a man's dollar, not because she thinks her work is unworthy of the full dollar, but because she's a member of the group of people who get pregnant and who are most implicated in child rearing. It means women would be expected to "invest" in child rearing in a country whose government does not seriously invest in child rearing. It means a woman would support spending on quality child care and quality public education, even if she doesn't have a child and never plans to have one—because it would make life better for both women and men.

If she is single, it means a woman would live a frugal life so that she need not resort to a man for financial survival, or to baby making as a trade or trade-off. If she also hopes to have children and work outside the home some day, financial independence enables the choosing of partners with good potential for sharing child-rearing duties.

If she is a primary caregiver and not working outside the home, it means a woman would appreciate the sacrifice of working women who are underpaid compared to men, and how that underpayment contributes to child rearing (for both her own and others' children). If she is a primary caregiver and employed, it means a woman would recognize that her role as a mother may take a toll on her performance as a worker or professional. It means acknowledging that women who are primary caregivers and employed are sometimes compromised by their roles and duties as mothers, and are not as able to excel in their jobs or careers as their colleagues (and forgiving herself for this). It means recognizing that things like morning sickness, breastfeeding, picking up kids on snow days, taking care of sick children, being sure there are meals for children to eat and clean clothes to wear, etc., often mitigate against the kind of excellence at work or in a career that gets a person big pay raises and promotions.

Taking one for the team also means being careful when assessing comparative gender statistics and asking critical questions (such as, "Why aren't there as many female district managers at this firm as there are male district managers?" or "Why are there more male full professors at this school than there are female full professors?"). Such care can help distinguish between real instances of sexism and other legitimate factors of discrimination. This kind of care seems especially appropriate if a woman enjoys additional income from a male partner, and so does not suffer as much from her 20-cent deflation as a single working woman or mother.

And finally, if she's good at her work, dedicated to her work, and can make it clear she's a no-kidder for life, then maybe a woman should be paid a full dollar for her work, and be promoted and recognized, not in an effort to bring about equity with men, or balance in numbers, but because the quality of her work calls for it.

The need for women in the United States to take one for the team and accept 80 cents for a dollar's worth of work is strong. Today, women are still responsible for the majority of day-to-day child care, and the results of efforts to get government, taxpayers, or others to constructively share this responsibility have been mixed. It's easy to assume that the U.S. political system will never substantially change, and that female biology is maternal, parental, and primary caregiver destiny. But we live in interesting times. Strong leadership, significant changes in attitudes, and shifts in public involvement in issues such as the balance of domestic vs. defense spending, health care, education, and child care are always possible, and if science eventually severs the link between reproduction and the female body, a whole new set of relations will be unleashed.[7]

# Sex and Politics

How does sex influence politics in the United States? How do male and female politicians negotiate this territory? What, for example, do we make of Bill Clinton's impeachment over an affair (an affair which was not his first)? Was it just a way to get him out of office, or did people really care about what he did sexually? And what do we make of politicians' infidelities, more generally?

What do we think of Hillary Clinton's elimination as a candidate for president in the 2008 Democratic primary? Was she discriminated against because of her sex? Was she more "in the running" in the first place because of her sex? It is useful to think about sex/gender and sexuality, and how they relate not only to politicians and their experiences in the past, but also to upcoming political contests, primaries, and presidential elections.

And why might it be that almost nobody commented when, in one of the last Democratic presidential primary debates of 2008, Clinton kept referring to Barack Obama by his first name, while Obama consistently called Clinton "Senator Clinton?" Was that sexist of her? And if the reverse had been the case—if Clinton had called Obama "Senator Obama" and Obama had called Clinton "Hillary"—would people have been more inclined to notice and be critical? This is just one example of an instance where sexism may have been identified, but wasn't. It suggests that the question "Is that sexist treatment?" is only part of the story. Also important is asking "When do accusations of sexism arise? Why are they made? and who gets to make them?[8]

Another thing to consider is why so few people commented on Hillary Clinton's tolerance of her husband's infidelities. Despite the widely celebrated cultural values of monogamy and fidelity, hardly anyone asked "Why didn't she get rid of Bill the first (or second, or third) time he cheated?" And why do so many political wives tolerate their husbands' infidelities? Unlike so many nonpolitical-spotlight wives, political wives have the financial and legal wherewithal to break off their marriages, and still retain a more-than-decent standard of living for themselves and their children. And what of those press conferences, with the cheating politician husbands, their lame apologies, and their stoical wives with the tight lips and blank stares? It's doubtful these couples are simply patching things over and putting on a brave face for the sake of the children. In smaller social groups, parents may be able to keep infidelity a secret or shield children from its more painful fallout. But the philandering activities of public figures quickly become the hot joke on multiple playgrounds for weeks and years to come. We are left with the sneaking suspicion that some political marriages have more to do with power and money than with love or intimacy, which would not be a problem in a less idealistic culture. But we live in an idealistic culture, and the idea of romantic love (or at least sexual fidelity) still plays a large part in people's ideas about what makes for a viable marriage and a well-lived life. Let's examine further why this is relevant to the voting public.

Americans have an awkward relationship to libido. Many love or admire the bad boy and the virile stud, but have a harder time reconciling the female Madonna (who is considered worthy of mothering children) with her counterpart, the whore. True to the double standard, many people are not as forgiving of the loose woman as they are of her male equivalent. Take Marion Barry, for instance, the mayor of Washington, D.C., who was reelected after he was caught with cocaine and prostitutes. Or John F. Kennedy, who also slept around while in office, as did a whole host of other U.S. presidents. In certain circumstances, a man may find it acceptable for a woman to sleep around, especially if he directly benefits from her availability. But he may not find this behavior so acceptable if the woman in question is his wife or daughter. Or it's OK for a woman to be a whore in the bedroom with her husband, but it's less OK for a woman to be a whore before marriage, or in any other context.

And what of the libido issue as it relates to women in politics? Can U.S. voters, like those in some European countries, find libidinous women political candidates appealing? Could they support a female political leader with a history of sexual "infractions" or a sexual wanderlust? Could conservative gender norms tolerate an adulterous female politician, or a single female politician with a yen for multiple lovers? Or are women held to higher moral standards? Are men, too, now being held to these higher standards? Or are these standards only selectively applied, when some change of political regime is desired?

It may be that women politicians in this country are left with only the sexless portion of virility and masculinity as it has been defined: the scrappy, "I'm-a-fighter" persona. Or it may be that people would be willing to tolerate a female candidate who has libido within her marriage, a woman who seems to enjoy and even relish her married life, including her married sexual life. The male version of this may be something that Obama supporters saw in his marital relations, and it was probably an advantage to him politically. Would the same have been true for a female candidate?

Or we might ask, is this the wrong approach entirely? Could people in the United States find a way, as they did in the past, to ignore or look past the private sexual lives of their leaders? Could they envision a form of strength that is not so sex linked—not so based on libido, virility, and machismo—but on something else entirely?

This love-hate relationship with libido inclines people to look for ways to wipe the slate clean when "selling" and "buying into" political candidates. It also helps explain the appeal of politicians who are born-again Christians—people who renounce their former "sinful selves" and pledge to reform their behavior. Born-again Christian voters may be more willing to accept this sort of renunciation (and these sorts of candidates) in the hope that the forgiveness favor will be returned.

We might also ask why it is that sometimes apologies are asked for, even for fairly small transgressions, while at other times, there seems to be no need to ask for forgiveness, even when serious transgressions have been made. Again, the question is not so much "Is that a transgression?" but "When do accusations of transgression arise? How do some transgressions compare to others? And when are apologies expected?" Consider honestly, which is worse: admitting to lusting over women and committing adultery in your heart or having a serious cocaine and/or prostitute-using habit? Which is worse: getting sexual favors in the Oval Office from an intern when your wife has already tolerated other infidelities, or promising the giver of those favors a comfortable taxpayer-supported government job as a reward for her "service?" Which is worse: deciding to forgive or tolerate a philandering husband, or acting like there is nothing at all wrong with having a philandering husband?

In the case of Hillary Clinton, putting up with a cheating husband may have acted both as a demerit for her as a politician, and as an invisible "sympathy card" (depending on the voter). Supporters of Hillary Clinton in the primaries included large numbers of working-class men (who are rather more comfortable with traditional gender roles, and perhaps more likely than progressives or idealistic voters to sympathize with or not be disturbed by the cheated-on wife). They also included women of the Gloria Steinem generation, who were mainly middle class, white, and liberal. Some of these women may have wanted to see Hillary Clinton in charge, so that finally a woman would be in control and have the ultimate say-so in the governmental "family."[9] The politics of "hurt feelings" also may have been a factor.[10] To put it bluntly, the presidency could have been seen as appeasement or compensation—a way for Hillary to get back at Bill, and a way for middle-class women to get back at their own philandering husbands, or make up for a lack of power in their own households and relationships.

Some people might like to think that electing a woman president would give the country a more feminine style of leadership, and focus attention on women's issues. Unfortunately, the tight association of feminine qualities and concerns with female bodies (and the denigration of these qualities) is problematic. Having breasts does make it possible to feed a baby (thankfully), but having breasts does not thereby ensure a more broadly nurturing or humane spirit. If it were the case that so called feminine characteristics were exclusive to women, many of the good ideas and policies our country has already embraced and enjoyed would not have come to pass.

Looking closely at gender stereotypes, such as women's caregiving and gentleness, or men's rationality and initiative, often reveals a difference of social situation or social expectation, and not a difference in innate capacities or essences. But even when deep differences do exist, there is still the general and uniquely human fear of death to consider. In anticipation of their own inevitable mortality, both men and women try to find ways to cope. Strategies of dealing with finitude include having and raising children; practices of meaningful work or artistic creation; service to a cause, idea, nation, or ideology, etc.[11]

The ways people deal with death can both constructive and destructive. But even if females, on average, design more constructive responses to the fact of death than males (because of their link with childbearing and "grounding" menstrual cycles), there is no guarantee that any individual woman would fit that statistic. Because women generally hold fewer and less prominent positions of public, political power than men, any negative responses they may have to the reality of death also would have less of an impact (e.g., a woman who "tortures" her children by forcing them to fulfill her own unfulfilled desires has less scope of impact than a man who sanctions the military of his country to torture an entire class of political prisoners, or eliminate an entire race of people). Of those women who have achieved significant leadership positions, some have been great, and others have done great damage.

These are just a few things to consider in the analyses of political races and careers when matters of sex and gender inevitably arise. As much as people would like to think so, neither sex is immune to the complexities of libido, and neither sex is innately better able to resist the attractions of power or the fear of death than the other. Any statistical differences we measure now in the way the sexes deal with problems have less to do with chromosomes and genes, and more to do with how we parcel out social duties. And regardless of these facts, statistical differences and the stereotypes they support would tell us little about the potential behavior of any one particular person—any one particular man or woman who might rise to a position of leadership and power. When it comes to politics, there are many variables relevant to voters' decisions, and many factors beyond voters' control that help determine elections. While the sexual energies and activities of politicians may be of some interest in the political process, the attention paid to sex and sexuality in politics often distracts citizens from far more significant and pressing matters of concern.

# Marriage

For middle-class heterosexuals in the United States (and for their counterparts in other industrialized countries), the question "why marry?" has become popular. Marriage was primarily designed as a way to enforce paternity, and is frequently defined as the proper context of child rearing. But today, marriage is less associated with both of these things, even in conservative neighborhoods when unintended pregnancies occur. As the cost of living increases, as populations soar, as pollution threatens health, as secure employment becomes scarce, and as the pain of sacrifice loses its status as a virtue, young people find fewer incentives for marriage, and more toward other activities that promise potential fulfillment (preserving or improving one's own standard of living, promoting a worthy cause, pursuing a career, etc.).

But in this country there are many reasons why marriage is a good idea. One is the heavily privatized health care system, which leads people to marry as a way to extend benefits (and decision-making rights) to both members of a relationship, and to ensure them for children who are either born into or brought into that family. Some people believe that children are better off when they are in the presence of two parents, one of each sex (each parent acting as a role model of that sex). Others have criticized this argument as heterosexist (and anti-communitarian). The value of an economy of scale, however, is seldom disputed. That is, it is easier if there are two providers or caregivers available to children in the primary family unit than if there is just one (and it may help with efforts to adopt). There is also the benefit of keeping the money in the family through shared assets, inheritance, tax advantages, and other benefits.

Marriage can also open new doors of social experience and meaning. Some people marry to make their love or existing commitment known and "official" to family, friends, their religious community and/or the broader community, and to gain the public and social support that married status offers. Another reason people marry has to do with citizenship, and explains why even people who are not interested in being sexual or procreative might marry as a way to prevent deportation, or help accomplish U.S. residency. The goodness of this last reason is, for some people, debatable.

In other cases, marriage is not a good idea. If women have good reasons to be gatekeepers of sexual relations, then men concerned with their emotional and financial well-being have good reasons to be gatekeepers of marriage. This is because women have a few additional "ethically suspect" reasons for getting married than do men. These reasons relate to women's slightly disadvantaged status in the United States (including the 80-cents-on-the-dollar issue) and biology. For example, if a woman is willing to marry solely because she (and her child/children/future children) needs financial security (or because she wants creature comforts), and if she has no feelings of either liking or love for her partner, then the marriage may run across difficulties, or fail to achieve even a baseline standard of marital intimacy and fulfillment.[12]

Other bad reasons for marriage include getting married because everyone else is doing it, getting married because that's what you're supposed to do, getting married so that on the wedding day you can dress up and boss everyone else around and be the center of attention, getting married so that someone will take care of you (do the laundry, cook the food, pay the bills, fix the gutters, and such), and getting married more for the opportunity to start sexual relations than for the opportunity to start the marital relationship itself.

Beyond the challenges that face all people, nothing precludes an unmarried person from loving others, caring for young people (as a volunteer, in that person's extended family, and so on), being an "economy of scale" with others in a household, getting help with housekeeping or home repair, dressing up and bossing people around, or taking part in a monogamous and fulfilling relationship. Still, doing these things instead of, or without, marrying can be seen (and experienced) as going against tradition, especially at certain times in life (such as young adulthood) and in certain contexts (as when one is in a healthy and monogamous relationship and others think it should go to the next stage). When in doubt, it is wise not to succumb to popular narratives or the peer pressure of others, and to marry only for good reasons.

# On Same-Sex Marriage

W hy do homosexual people (gay men and lesbians) want to marry? And why is it that some straight (and even some non-straight) people do not want gays or lesbians to marry? Obviously, marriage is a powerful institution that affords substantial rights on a couple. It creates families, and confers social, economic, and health care benefits. It is also a complex intersection of religion and state.

Some lesbians and gay men have argued against same-sex marriage. They say marriage has been so corrupted by straight couples and by religion, that buying into its practice would be a mistake. But others argue that the legitimacy and rights conferred by marriage are too desirable to swear off, and that marriage is a sacred vow without substitute (that is to say, a civil union is not enough). Some also argue that gay and lesbian couples help restore the image of marriage, and help assert its significance and desirability by confirming the importance of monogamy, and adding to the total number of happily married couples.[13]

Because health care in the United States is still significantly privatized, there is incentive for people to find jobs with good health benefits. There is also incentive to marry, so as to get the best possible employee health benefits for or from spouses and for children, especially if only one member of a parenting couple is employed outside the home. This health care situation means that there are more reasons to marry in this country than there are in countries where health care is less tied (or not at all tied) to the private sector, employment, or marital status. It also means that in addition to the more spiritual and social reasons for marriage, gays and lesbians in the United States would be interested in marrying for health benefits as well.

Those who do not support same-sex marriage do so for as many reasons as those who support it. Some are motivated by a revulsion encouraged by the culture, one that is largely unexamined and unexplained. Because being "not feminine" or "not gay" plays such a prominent role in popular notions of U.S. masculinity, hostility toward gay males is a convenient means of scapegoating—projecting undesirable qualities onto a class of individual who are "others," and who can then be easily denigrated. This form of keeping up with the Joneses is powerful as long as it has momentum.

People uncomfortable with sex acts practiced by some homosexuals may not realize that some straight couples also do these things. They may associate these acts with bad experiences, or they may be unhappy about the fact that they may not get to participate in these acts, but would really like to. At the same time, same-sex sexual activity in the animal world has been largely overlooked or downplayed by biologists and evolutionary theorists.[14]

Then there are those in psychology and religion who have told people that homosexuality is wrong or unnatural. Often, their arguments rest on the claim that all sex should at least mirror procreative sex. If people who make this argument also believe that surrogate parenting, in vitro fertilization, masturbation, and oral sex are unethical, they at least would be consistent. Frequently, however, people are idiosyncratically selective about what kinds of "unnatural" acts they find acceptable, and what kinds they don't.

Religious arguments against homosexuality relate to other religious beliefs about sexuality. For example, many religions believe celibacy is the highest sexual virtue, and expect or demand it of their spiritual leaders. In this case, any sex—straight or gay—is seen as a distraction from holiness or transcendence. But others argue that celibacy is just another form of denial, and no more likely to lead its practitioners to goodness, love, or God.[15]

In the early Christian Church, St. Thomas Aquinas established a strict form of one-man-one-woman marriage as the foundation of the Christian family, not because it resulted in children, but because it was the least unsatisfactory way to keep the species going while "containing" worse forms of fornication.[16] In subsequent years, the Latin Church forbade priests and cloistered nuns to marry, and built all-male monasteries. Taboos against homosexuality may have been an attempt to keep religious leaders, monks, nuns, and clergy away from same-sex temptations of the flesh, but mandates of abstinence do not always hold sway.[17] Needless to say, in many religions, mixed feelings remain about bodies, purity, sexuality, and the place of materiality in the realms of spirituality and transcendence. Whether or not a religion will be able to think of homosexuality as natural, or as a viable marital relation, depends on a whole host of variables, doctrines, and historical precedent.

Some people fear that same-sex marriage further separates marriage from procreation, and further distances family arrangements from blood relations, especially paternity (this is already the case with adoption and blended families). The consequences of such distancing are not altogether clear, and people are often afraid of the unknown. Some worry that a slippery slope would result. In other words, if same-sex marriage were acceptable, would polygamous (one man, many wives), polyandrous (one wife, many husbands), or polyamorous (multiple partners) arrangements also demand recognition as viable family arrangements? Would these new arrangements be going too far, or be too difficult for the state to negotiate? Would there be benefits to recognizing these new arrangements? Would problems with these new arrangements outweigh the benefits?

If only love and choice make a marriage and not children, then some people worry about what might happen to paternity and fatherhood and the place of men in society. Would men grow into new kinds of fathers? Would the patriarchal nuclear family break down even further than it already has? What social institutions, if any, would help make up for the patriarchal nuclear family and the role men play in them?

One interesting finding is that many straight people who oppose same-sex marriage also thoroughly embrace and encourage traditional gender roles. These roles—roles such as male breadwinner and female caregiver and homemaker—are associated with middle-class patriarchal nuclear families, and are not natural categories of activity. From studying other cultures and various economic classes, we know that it is not necessarily (or only) the man of the house who is the wage earner or food provider. Nor are cooking, cleaning, and child rearing always a mother's tasks. Yet it is people who are comfortable with (and feel they benefit from) these traditional roles who more acutely feel they have something to lose if marriages between two people of the same sex are allowed. This is because same-sex marriage makes it concretely evident that no one sex "deserves" or "owns" or "should perform" any particular set of duties.

Religion is older than the nation-state, and tribes and religions invented marriage before governments got involved. This does not mean, however, that marriage is only a religious matter. Groups, tribes, and cultures have trafficked in women for a variety of political, social, and economic reasons. When organized religions grew to power, they laid claim to authorizing this practice. Today, the state does, too. So who owns marriage now—religion, or the state? The answer is both. And this presents a problem for a country that prides itself on the separation of church and state.

Civil unions are one response to this problem. A civil union is a form of marriage in the legal sense, but not in the religious sense. Granting civil unions might avoid some of the resistance that same-sex marriage inspires, but may be seen as inferior by gays and lesbians who want to be recognized as married (and not just united in a civil sense), or who are part of a religion that would recognize same-sex marriage.

Creating civil unions might also have a proliferating effect on marriage. If civil unions were offered, not just to same-sex couples, but to everyone as an alternative to marriage (or in addition to a religious marriage), heterosexual couples might opt for it instead of a religious marriage, same-sex couples might opt for it, or same-sex couples might opt for it *and* have a marriage ceremony in a sympathetic religion. People might specify what *kind* of marriage they have, or be more likely to identify themselves as married in some way or other in order to reflect political leanings (for instance, "I'm a married Catholic" vs. "I'm a married Unitarian" vs. "I'm in a civil union"). "Are you single or married?" is a question that would no longer end discussion; it would start one. This is why some people argue that people who are interested in preserving the institution of marriage would be wise to grant gays and lesbians the right to marry—because granting the alternative, civil unions, would have this deconstructing effect. Whether an explosion of marital denominations would be seen as an improvement of marriage or as the dissolution of its essence would largely depend upon the perspective of the person making the assessment and the communities in which they take part.

## Endnotes

1. John D'Emilio and Estelle B. Freedman, 1988.
2. For more on the relationship between fathers, the nuclear family, and the state, see Bertrand Russell, *Marriage and Morals*, 1957.
3. For more on ethically informed no-kidders, see Lisa Hymas's discussion of GINKs: Green Inclined - No Kids, www.grist.org.
4. Martha Nussbaum, 1999.
5. This question about work and pay should be considered in its historical context. As Dorothy Sayers outlined in *Are Women Human?* (1971), women's work has changed over the years in England and the United States. Much of what women used to do in the home (spinning, dyeing, weaving, brewing, distilling, preserving, pickling, bottling, curing meat, and so forth) has been taken over by industry since around the turn of the last century. The loss of these integral economic functions (which could be done in the home while simultaneously caring for and teaching small children), is part of the story of women's work, as is today's heavy reliance on wage work, and the proliferation of large-scale corporations with significant control in manufacturing, service, education, and information.
6. George F. Gilder, 1973.
7. Shulamith Firestone, 1970.
8. Corey Anton and Valerie V. Peterson, 2003.
9. For more on how the government is understood of in terms of family, see George Lakoff's *Moral Politics: What Conservatives Know That Liberals Don't*, 1996.

10. This is an expression Vivian Gornick uses to describe some feminists' motives in her introduction to Erving Goffman's book, *Gender Advertisements*, 1974.
11. See Ernest Becker's *Denial of Death*, 1973.
12. In cultures and subcultures characterized by arranged marriages, this more pragmatic approach to marriage may not be a problem.
13. David Brooks, 2003.
14. Joan Roughgarden, 2004.
15. Jiddu Krishnamurti, 1969.
16. See Baker and Elliston's Introduction to *Philosophy and Sex*, 1975.
17. Curb and Manahan, 1985.

# Appendix A

Euphemisms and Alternative Wording Suggestions

*I would like to have sex now/soon.*

> Conventional nonverbal gestures or signs (including theatrical or contextual cues) indicating interest in or willingness to have sex (perhaps a kind of touch, a specific candle or lamp lit, particular music played, special undergarments, etc.).
>
> Any of the many other verbal and nonverbal ways of making the invitation ("Want to fool around?").
>
> A couple's own invented gestures, signs, words, or code phrases.

*I don't feel like having sex right now.*

> I really like you/love you, but can I take a rain check?
>
> I can do this other sexually intimate practice—would that work for you?
>
> I can handle a "quickie" (brief intercourse), but you'll have to do the "work of the man."[1]

I feel resentful and upset about such-and-such, and that feeling is getting in the way of me feeling OK about having sex. Can we talk about it, so I can get past it?

I really enjoy having sex with you, but right now …

—I don't have birth control available or I missed a pill; let's wait.

—I think I may have a minor bacterial or yeast infection. Can we wait until my symptoms subside?

—I'm just too tired/preoccupied/busy/overwrought by work-related concerns.

—My gut is messed up from lunch, and I don't trust my digestive tract.

—I just drank a lot of water and it will slosh. Can we wait a half hour?

(In whatever way seems appropriate, confirm your affection for your partner, then give an honest explanation.)

*I don't like what you're doing. (attend to tone of voice here)*

Here, do this ….

That's a bit too far/gentle/hard/painful/uncomfortable/direct. Can we do this? … Can you try this?

Can we change positions? Can I move this way a little?

*I can't figure out what you want me to do. (attend to tone of voice here)*

What do you like? What would you like me to do?

Do you like this?

Is "this" better than "that?"

*You smell bad.*

Let's take a shower together.

Why don't you take a shower, while I get started without you?

How about we try a different (or such-and-such) position? Or simply, can we do xyz position?

*You're pulling my hair.*

My hair is caught.

## Endnotes

1. "The "work of the man" is mentioned in the *Kama Sutra*. It describes the "work" of the person—male or female—who is on top during sex.

# Appendix B

## Sex Inventory

(Responses to these questions should be updated periodically.)

Are you physically and emotionally ready for (possible consequences of) the physical intimacies in which you plan to engage?

Are you clear and honest with yourself and your sexual partner about what sexual intimacy means to you and to your partner? (Do you love your partner? Do you like your partner? Do you know anything about your partner? How does this factor in for you?)

Are there any concerns about either participant's sexual history that need to be addressed?

If you anticipate intercourse, but do not wish to conceive, are you using, or do you have access to, a reliable form or forms of birth control?

If you cannot be fairly sure of monogamy and a clean bill of health regarding STDs, are you using a condom to help protect against sexually transmitted disease?

Are there any bad experiences in your past that may shape the way you react to certain aspects of sexual intimacy? If so, can you explain enough about this so that problems can be avoided?

Do you take any medications, or have any medical or physical conditions that may negatively affect you sexually? If so, can you explain how are you affected, and what might be done to mitigate any negative effects?

Excluding intercourse, what are the different varieties of sexual intimacies that you are willing to do or are interested in or capable of doing?

What are the different varieties of sexual positions that you are willing to do or are interested in or capable of doing?

What sexual acts do you feel you'd really not want to experiment with?

What are your sexual turn-ons? (What kinds of things get you in the mood for sex? Specifically, what kinds of things do you like your partner to do?)

What are your sexual turn-offs? (What kinds of things undermine your interest in having sex? Specifically, what kinds of things would you rather your partner not do?)

How do you feel about menstruation and sexual intimacy?

Ideally, how much sexual intimacy would you have every day, week, or month? What kinds of intimacy might this include?

What is your favorite time of day to have sex?

What times of day do you not like to have sex?

What sort of setting do you find ideal for sex?

# Works Cited

Anton, C., and Peterson, V. V. (2003). Who said what: Subject positions, rhetorical strategies, and good faith. *Communication Studies*, 54 (4), 403–419.

Baker, R., and Elliston, F. (eds.). (1975). *Philosophy and Sex*. New York: Prometheus Books.

Baker, R. (1975). Pricks and chicks: A plea for "persons." In Baker R., and Elliston, F. (eds.), *Philosophy and Sex* (pp. 45–64). New York: Prometheus Books.

Becker, E. (1973). *The Denial of Death*. New York: Free Press.

Berger, A. A. (1998). *Seeing Is Believing: An Introduction to Visual Communication* (2nd ed.). Mountain View, CA: Mayfield.

Borowitz, E. B. (1969). *Choosing a Sex Ethic: A Jewish Inquiry*. New York: Schocken Books.

Brooks, D. (2003, November 22). *The power of marriage*. New York Times, http://selectnytimes.com/search/restricted/article/res=F40C1FFE385.

Butler, J. (1993). *Bodies That Matter: On The Discursive Limits Of "Sex."* New York: Routledge.

Catania, J. A. (1999). A framework for conceptualizing reporting bias and its antecedents in interviews assessing human sexuality. *Journal of Sex Research*, 36 (1), 25–38.

Curb, R., and Manahan, N. (eds.). (1985). *Lesbian Nuns Breaking Silence*. Tallahassee, FL: Naiad Press.

D'Emilio, J., and Freedman, E. B. (1988). *Intimate Matters: A History of Sexuality in America*. New York: Harper & Row.

Firestone, S. (1970). *The Dialectics of Sex: The Case for Feminist Revolution*. New York: William Morrow.

Fromm, E. (1956). *The Art of Loving*. New York: Harper & Row.

Foucault, M. (1978). *The History of Sexuality* (R. Hurley, trans.). New York: Random House. (Original work published 1976).

Fuss, D. (1989). *Essentially Speaking: Feminism, Nature and Difference*. New York: Routledge.

Gilder, G. F. (1973). *Sexual Suicide*. New York: Quadrangle.

Goffman, E. (1974). *Gender advertisements. Studies in the Anthropology of Visual Communication*, 3 (2), 295–xxx.

Gornick, V. (1974). Introduction. *Studies in the Anthropology of Visual Communication*, 3 (2), 292–294.wGray, J. (1995). *Mars and Venus in the Bedroom: A Guide to Lasting Romance and Passion*. New York: Harper Collins.

Grosz, E. (1994). *Volatile Bodies: Toward a Corporeal Feminism*. Bloomington: Indiana University Press.

James, W. (1958). *Talks to Teachers on Psychology and to Students on Some of Life's Ideals*. New York: W. W. Norton & Co.

Jonas, H. (1979). *The Phenomenon of Life: Toward a Philosophical Biology*. Chicago: University of Chicago Press.

Katz, J. N. (1996). *The Invention of Heterosexuality*. New York: Plume.

Krishnamurti, J. (1953). *Education and the Significance of Life*. New York: HarperCollins.

Krishnamurti, J. (1969). *Freedom from the Known*. San Francisco: Harper & Row.

Lakoff, G. (1996). *Moral Politics: What Conservatives Know That Liberals Don't*. Chicago: University of Chicago Press.

Lakoff, G., and Johnson, M. (1980). *Metaphors We Live By*. Chicago: University of Chicago Press.

Leder, D. (1990). *The Absent Body*. Chicago: University of Chicago Press.

MacDougall, R. (2006). Remaking the real man: Erectile dysfunction palliatives and the social reconstruction of the male heterosexual life cycle. *Sexuality & Culture*, 10 (3), 59–90.

Masters, W. H., and Johnson, V. E. (1966). *Human Sexual Response.* New York: Bantam Books.

Noble, D. (1992). *A World Without Women: The Christian Clerical Culture of Western Science.* New York: Oxford University Press.

Nussbaum, M. C. (1986). *The Fragility of Goodness: Luck and Ethics in Greek Tragedy and Philosophy.* New York: Cambridge University Press.

Nussbaum, M. C. (1999). *Sex and Social Justice.* New York: Oxford University Press.

Peterson, V. V. (on press). Sex drug technologies: A media ecological approach to birth control and ed drugs. In MacDougall, R. (ed.), *Drugs and Media: New Perspectives on Communication, Consumption and Consciousness* (in press). New York: Continuum.

Peterson, V. V. (2010). Birth control: An extension of "man." *Explorations in Media Ecology* 9 (1), 1-20.

Peterson, V. V. (2008). The sex of joy: A gourmet guide to lovemaking rhetoric. *Popular Communication,* 6 (1), 1–17.

Peterson, V. V. (2005). "Ellen": Coming out and disappearing. In Dalton, M. M., and Linder, L. R. (eds.), *America Viewed and Skewed: Television Situation Comedies* (pp. 165–176). New York: State University of New York (SUNY).

Peterson, V. V. (2002). Text as cultural antagonist: The Kama sutra of Vatsyayana. *Journal of Communication Inquiry,* 26 (2), 133–154.

Peterson, V. V. (2001). The rhetorical criticism of visual elements: An alternative to Foss's schema. *Southern Communication Journal,* 67 (1), 19–32.

Peterson, V. V. (2000). Mars and Venus: The rhetoric of sexual planetary alignment. *Women & Language,* 23 (2), 1–8.

Peterson, V. V. (1999). *Sex Texts: The Social Construction of Sex in Popular Manuals,* 1962–1995. Unpublished doctoral dissertation, University of Iowa, Iowa City.

Peterson, V. V. (1998). Sexual Politics. In Amico, E. B. (ed.), *Reader's Guide to Women's Studies* (pp. 552–553). Chicago: Fitzroy Dearborn.

Peterson, V. V. (1997). Beyond dichotomy: The sophists' understanding of antithetical thought. *Advances in the History of Rhetoric,* 1 (1), 1–8.

Plato. (1956). *Phaedrus* (W. C. Helmbold, W. G. Rabinowitz, trans.). New York: Macmillan.

Poulakos, J., and Poulakos, T. (1999). *Classical Rhetorical Theory*. Boston: Houghton Mifflin.

Reeder, H. (1996). A critical look at gender difference in communication research. *Communication Studies*, 47 (4), 318–330.

Rich, A. (2004). Compulsory heterosexuality and lesbian existence. *In Blood, Bread, and Poetry*. New York: Norton Paperback.

Roughgarden, J. (2004). *Evolution's Rainbow*. Berkeley: University of California Press.

Royce, J. (1967). *Perception, conception, and interpretation. In The Problem of Christianity* (pp. 109–163). New York: Archon Books.

Rubin, L. B. (1990). *Erotic Wars: What Happened to the Sexual Revolution?* New York: Farrar, Straus & Giroux.

Russell, B. (1970). *Marriage and Morals*. New York: Liveright Publishing Corporation.

Sayers, D. L. (1971). *Are Women Human?* Grand Rapids, MI: William B. Eerdmans Publishing Co.

Shlain, L. (2003). *Sex, Time and Power: How Women's Sexuality Shaped Human Evolution*. New York: Viking Press.

Solomon, R. C. (1981). *Love: Emotion, Myth, and Metaphor*. Garden City, New York: Anchor Press.

Vatsyayana (1964). *The Kama Sutra of Vatsyayana* (R. F. Burton, trans.). New York: E. P. Dutton.